To Joel —
Great Success!
with your books!
— Marily

MARKETING
YOUR BOOKS

A Collection of Profit-Making Ideas for Authors and Publishers

Marilyn and Tom Ross

**COMMUNICATION
CREATIVITY**
425 Cedar Street
Buena Vista, CO 81211

Although the authors and publisher have made every effort to ensure the accuracy and completeness of information contained in this book, we assume no responsibility for errors, inaccuracies, omissions, or any inconsistency herein. Any slights of people or organizations are unintentional.

Library of Congress Cataloging-in-Publication Data

Ross, Marilyn Heimberg.
   Marketing your books : a collection of profit-making ideas for authors and publishers / by Marilyn and Tom Ross.
     p.   cm.
   Includes index.
   ISBN 0-918880-21-1 : $9.95
   1. Books—Marketing. 2. Authors and publishers. 3. Publishers and publishing. I. Ross, Tom, 1933- . II. Title.
Z283.R67 1989
070.5'93068'8—dc19   89-7259
                                               CIP

Acknowledgment

We wish to thank our clients for the inspiration to do this book. They challenged us to constantly find new and better ways to market their books.

We are also indebted to Alley DeVore, whose sensitive editing added to the clarity of our message.

Contents

Introduction

We live in a publishing era where big names write big books that are promoted with big dollars. But where does that leave those of us whose name isn't Ludlum, Steel, Kowalski, Clancy, Dailey, Trump, or a handful of others? In the middle of Nowhereville, that's where.

The March 1, 1988, issue of the *Wall Street Journal* reported, "Best-selling books are made, not born. Authors are starting to grasp this simple fact. Now, as publishers increasingly invest most of their promotion budgets in a few big books, many authors are paying large sums to hire personal publicists." Let's be realistic and acknowledge the facts: if you're not a household word, your publisher will typically allocate scant time and a minuscule budget to market your title.

The encouraging news is that's no reason to be discouraged. There are proven ways you can keep that tight budget from cramping your style. You—yes *you*—can have a profound impact on the sale of your book! That's what this volume is all about. You don't need to hire a personal publicist; you can become one!

It doesn't pretend to cover every conceivable marketing ploy, although the "Ross Idea Generator" lists 44 winning strategies. What it does do is present an in-depth examination of a baker's dozen sure-fire approaches. You'll discover how to use radio to sell books from your home or office, open up special sales opportunities, and capitalize on free book promotion. Also covered is merchandising serial rights, positioning your books as premiums, focusing attention via newspaper op-ed pages, selling to book clubs, and creating a customer brochure to stimulate more sales.

In the chapter on "Editorial Tactics to Increase Your Marketing Edge," authors (and editors) discover why they should be thinking about marketing at the onset of any book project. Those considering writing about a specific area will find "Regional Publishing Can Pay Big Dividends" of particular interest.

There are also two interviews with the Rosses reprinted from publishing industry newsletters. These reveal penetrating answers to difficult questions. The book concludes with a unique chapter that shows writers how to use their time more profitably.

Who is *Marketing Your Books: A Collection of Profit-Making Ideas for Authors and Publishers* written for? ALL authors. You'll need it for sure if you're a mid-list, non-celebrity writer published by a major New York house. And while smaller independent presses often spend more energy and time on promoting their titles, most will love you for your help. Those who choose to self-publish their work will find ideas here to fund their ventures, not to mention lucrative ongoing strategies. Savvy people in this latter group—entrepreneurs at heart—know that sound marketing goes hand in hand with success.

Surprisingly, traditional publishers can also benefit from *Marketing Your Books*. This is the grist from a working mill. It presents proven concepts—but ones often ignored by the establishment. It is both an ideal text for interns, and offers personnel in commercial book publicity departments a fresh look at the options available for shrewd book promotion.

Getting into print is only the beginning. Today—with some 53,000 new books churned out each year—it's publicize or perish. Effective promotion and opening national channels of distribution are vital. If you're like most people, however, this can be as intimidating as meeting your future mother-in-law. It requires unique know-how. A creative mindset. Innovation. That's what is waiting for you in the following pages.

1

Editorial Tactics to Increase Your Marketing Edge

In today's competitive world of publishing, smart authors and publishers start thinking "marketing" when they first begin a book project. Sound like a lopsided statement? Not really. There are things you can add as you shape and create the manuscript that will furnish additional clout when it comes time to sell that book.

Adding Chapters for Greater Diversity

The more promotional angles you provide for your book, the more sales will mushroom. You widen the book's appeal by thinking through your topic and slanting parts of it to different audiences. One reason this is a shrewd approach is that magazines and newspapers often buy what are called serial or excerpt rights. That means they purchase a small portion of your book to run in their publication. (We show you how to sell to them in a later chapter.) Even though the overall thrust of your message might not be applicable, they may find a section, chapter, or quiz that appeals to their particular readers. Such exposure can be crucial in bringing your title to the attention of thousands of extra people and stimulating word-of-mouth sales.

Let's suppose you have a book on alcoholism. Have you included a chapter on teenage alcoholics? This will open a whole new niche for marketing the book to schools, professional counselors, even progressive churches. What about a chapter for the mate of an alcoholic? Adding such information could turn a book that has no appeal to women's magazines into one they would consider reviewing or excerpting.

Maybe your title is *The Second Time Around*. Besides the usual focus on how to meet someone and develop a good relationship, probe deeper. How about a chapter on dealing harmoniously with ex-spouses? What about advice on visiting arrangements for grandparents when normal family ties no longer exist? Wouldn't a section on handling hostile step-children be useful to many?

Look for ways to give your book more universal appeal. There is no lay person's book on how to produce, package and market cassette tapes. Let's pretend we're doing one. When developing the Table of Contents think about the kinds of people who might use such a book. Publishers to be sure. But what about a separate chapter for aspiring musicians? And how about specific sections for ministers—speakers—trainers—authors—sales managers—politicians—even meeting planners who are often responsible for making arrangements to tape conventions? Thus a book that might appeal only to publishers is expanded to many potential markets.

Putting in Strategic Editorial "Zingers"

There are other things you can do at the writing stage to boost sales later. Sometimes it makes a lot of sense to mention key places or people.

When Marilyn wrote her first book back in 1978, she tried to sell it to the bookstore at Cabrillo National Monument in San Diego, the most visited of all historic sites in the U.S. Their answer was no; the book had no relationship to the monument, they said. She filed this away for future reference. When writing *Creative Loafing* a year later, guess which national monument was prominently featured in this guide of leisure pursuits? Sure enough, they took the bait and carried the book.

In *How to Make Big Profits Publishing City and Regional Books*, we share hundreds of specific anecdotes and book titles. They show how broad this specialty publishing field actually is. When making the Index, we listed each book that was referred to. Then we used the Index to help prepare a special mini-mailing to the publishers covered. It cited the page number each was mentioned on and suggested purchasing a copy of the book. The orders rolled in. One marketing director even sent along this note: "Enclosed is our order for a copy of your new book. We received your flier and I do want to congratulate you on a clever and effective marketing technique." You can use this tip to increase your sales as well.

Front and Back Matter as Sales Stimulators

Most people wouldn't think that the front and back matter–those things that come before and after the main text in a book–would have much bearing on how it sells. Not so. This material can have a dramatic impact on your book's success! First, let's consider front matter.

One of the more creative things you can do to strengthen your position is to get a person recognized in the field you're dealing with to write a Foreword. When Don Dible published *Up Your Own Organization* several years ago, few people knew who he was. Businesspeople did recognize the names of Robert Townsend, who turned Avis around, and William Lear, head of Lear Motors Corporation. Dible got Townsend to write an Introduction to his book and Lear to do the Foreword. Then he splashed *their names* on the cover of his book and in the promotional material to give his project credibility.

Physicians, attorneys, and certain other professionals can be tapped for Forewords. They are usually thrilled to get their names on book covers. And there may be an additional benefit for you: a doctor, for instance, will read your manuscript for accuracy as well, because he or she would be embarrassed by errors.

Under Acknowledgments is another place to mention key names—not only of those you genuinely wish to thank for their help, but also of people you want to favor and impress. Sometimes they will be so flattered to be singled out they will help promote your book by recommending it to others. Such word-of-mouth endorsements are like money in the bank.

Have you ever gone to a bookstore and watched browsers? First they look at the front cover. Then if the book still holds their attention, they turn it over and examine the back cover. The next thing they'll usually do is flip to the Table of Contents and either make a buying decision—or move on to another book.

Therein lies a profound revelation: the Table of Contents is one of your most valuable sales tools! Make it meaty. Exciting. Benefit-oriented. Include the subheads as well as the chapter titles. Tell potential buyers specifically what the book delivers, using punchy phraseology and active verbs. Notice the adjacent sample.

If the book will be rolling off the press at the end of the year, use the *next year* in your copyright notice. Thus it will seem fresh for a much longer time and have a better crack at continuing reviews. This ploy is used even by major publishers. A top executive at one of the biggest trade houses confided to us that they routinely do this with any book coming out after September.

Other important things every self-publisher should have includes an ISBN. This number—obtained from the R. R. Bowker Company, 249 W. 17th Street, New York, NY 10011—is to a book what your social security number is to you. CIP is also important. CIP stands for Cataloging in Publication and aids librarians in shelving your book more quickly and inexpensively.

Now let's examine some of the ingredients that come after the main part of the book and can mean extra dollars in your pocket.

Fat Appendices really pay off. In fact, some people buy a book solely because of the unique reference information presented in the Appendix. Also if your book contains enough data, it may qualify for a listing in *Directory of Directories in Print*. We had a client several years back who had written an autobiographical expose decrying slipshod

TABLE OF CONTENTS

medical practices. Her topic lent itself to listings of various associations dealing with specific diseases, consumer medical advocacy groups, state medical policing agencies, et cetera. We counseled her to add these additional sources of information in the Appendix to increase the book's worth. That way her autobiography became a "reference work" because it included a compendium of valuable resources not previously collected in one place.

Adding a Glossary can also be a smart move, especially if you use a lot of unfamiliar terms. Our *Complete Guide to Self-Publishing* was recently reviewed by John Kremer in *Small Press* magazine. One of the things he said was, "The Rosses have defined over 400 publishing terms in a separate Glossary, *an indispensable reference resource for neophytes.*" Sometimes people who need to know the terminology of a certain industry will buy your book strictly for the Glossary!

A nonfiction book without an Index is like bread without butter. Readers want—and deserve—to be able to locate specific pieces of information quickly. The only way they can do that is through an Index. Librarians expect them; educational sales will be sadly dampened for a book that lacks one. (And as we pointed out earlier, indexes can also serve as a marketing tool for you to pinpoint individuals or groups who might be interested in purchasing your book.)

Last, but certainly not least, should be an Order Form. It amazes us how seldom books include this obvious sales opportunity. How often do you use a library book—and later want to purchase a personal copy? Or borrow a book from a friend—then want one yourself? Our philosophy is make it easy to buy!

At Communication Creativity we get many orders every week on the order forms we provide in the backs of our books.

Design it as an actual Order Form—complete with lines for name, address, city, state, zip, and phone number. If you offer credit card purchasing, include logos for the various cards, a place for the card number, expiration date, and a signature line. Compute the state sales tax and express it in exact dollars and cents rather than a percentage. Add a postage and shipping fee. (With the recent rise in postage, we typically recommend $2-$3 per book.) Remember to highlight offers for discounts on quantity orders. You do give them, don't you? This form should appear on the next to last page of the book. It's easy to see there. And if readers tear it out, they won't be ripping out part of the Index or other important material. Most people simply photocopy it, however.

The ideas we've been sharing are guaranteed to hike the sales of your books. But these things must be done early in the writing process. Good marketing planning begins when you first start thinking about the shape of a manuscript. By employing the strategies we've discussed at that early stage, you're assured of stronger sales throughout the life of your book.

Now let's move ahead and explore how you can get more than your share of promotion and media attention.

2

Capitalizing on Free Book Promotion and Media Opportunities

PR is the ideal marketing tool every astute author or publisher uses. It can give an enormous boost for virtually no cost to those who don't have ad budgets approaching the size of General Motors. Any author is wise to promote his or her own book, even if it is trade published. One client wrote us, "I make twice the money promoting and selling my own book as I do on royalties."

Promotion starts a chain reaction. People begin to hear about your book, read about it, see it, buy it, tell others about it. This promotes word-of-mouth advertising. It's like yeast; sales expand rapidly when the book world begins to talk about your title. Beautiful *free* publicity, more than anything else, is what stimulates this fermentation process. Here's how to get it started.

PRing Key Individuals

By beginning on a local level, you can generate a ripple effect that will carry you regionally, then nationally. A little thinking will quickly reveal several influential locals who should receive a complimentary copy of your book. Start your list with the book review editor of the largest daily—and deliver his or her copy personally. What about smaller papers and regionally oriented magazines? Contact the main branch librarian responsible for acquisitions in your subject area. Once you've convinced this individual you have a good book, many branch libraries will probably order.

Would adding the honcho at the visitor and convention bureau or your chamber of commerce be of any value? What about area politicians? A publisher of a tourist guide told us one of her best channels of distribution is legislators who use her book as a giveaway to visiting dignitaries. She lobbied them extensively when her book first came out. By all means, hand deliver an autographed copy to the mayor.

Depending on the nature of your publication, think about others with special interests who would appreciate having a copy. They will often be excellent goodwill ambassadors. These people may provide advance comments you can use to catapult the book to wider acclaim, plus favorably impact sales by recommending it to colleagues.

Creating Events

Creating an "event" is another excellent way to focus attention on your book. Vicki Morgan of San

Francisco's Foghorn Press did this in spades for their
first title, *Forty Niners: Looking Back* by Joseph
Hession. To launch it, Foghorn teamed up with the
Pro Football Hall of Fame to stage a media event
that would tie in with the 49ers' 40th year. It also
coincided with the book's arrival from the printers.
The gala evening was held at no less than the pres-
tigious Mark Hopkins Intercontinental Hotel on Nob
Hill. It featured former and current members of the
San Francisco 49ers, hosted cocktails and hors
d'oeuvres, door prizes, NFL films, music, entertainment, and—of course—a copy of the book. Tickets
sold for a hefty $65. Three hundred people at-
tended.

While Morgan wanted the party to draw fans, her
main priority was to capture media attention. Thirty-
one members of the media showed up, including all
three major local TV stations. Radio KSJO covered
the party live. The bottom line, of course, is what
matters. *Forty Niners: Looking Back* came out the
beginning of December. By the end of the month,
8,000 copies had been sold! Foghorn now is recognized as a fresh new force in the publishing community and has valuable contacts with sports writers
and editors throughout the Bay Area.

We did something similar back in 1978 for *Creative Loafing*. We joined forces with the Aerospace
Museum in San Diego and presented "Creative
Loafing Days" in Balboa Park. Portraying the shoe-
string leisure activities depicted in the book, we had
clowns, a frog jumping jamboree, and poetry readings. Other festivities included a jousting match by
the Society of Creative Anachronism, plus demonstrations by mountain men, martial arts pros, and
fencing experts. Because the museum was a non-

profit organization, we qualified for dozens of free PSA (public service announcement) radio commercials spotlighting the event and mentioning the book title. Not only did Creative Loafing Days hit all three TV networks, and our publishing company receive a commendation from the mayor, we also sold out the hardcover print run.

Books which cover timely issues or are highly controversial may warrant a press conference. If you plan to call an official press conference, here are a few tips: Choose a time and place that is convenient for the media. Mornings are best; there will be less competition Tuesday through Thursday. Double-check on the possibility of any other important conflicting function, such as the arrival of the Pope or a political announcement by an important legislator, that would cut your attendance to a trickle. Arrange for news releases to arrive about a week before the event. Try to create something visually exciting so TV camera crews will have a real reason for showing up.

It's a good idea to place follow-up calls a couple of days before the conference to be sure appropriate people know about it (and as a subtle reminder). At the event itself, have media kits and refreshments available, give out books lavishly, deliver a short well-prepared talk, answer any questions, and be your most charming self.

Media Opportunities

Producers and hosts at area radio, TV, newspapers, and magazines can be some of your best friends...*if* you approach them right!

First, you need to determine who's out there and how to reach them. Many larger metropolitan areas sport their own media directories. There are *New York Publicity Outlets, Southern California Media Director, Washington News Media Directory* and *FinderBinders* in various cities. Of course, one of the national media directories located in the reference section of your library will provide intriguing possibilities all across the U.S. Correspondence should be directed *by name* to the producer of a radio or TV show—to the section editor of a newspaper (Scene/Sports/Business, et cetera)—or to the managing editor of a magazine. If it's impossible to get a name, at least use the person's appropriate title.

Once you've made up a list of the likely places to get publicity, it's time to create a dynamite media kit. (That's a subject all by itself, one covered in dozens of publicity manuals.) Of course, for your prime contacts you'll also automatically include a book. Lesser lights get a copy if they indicate interest and request one. Plan on working far ahead, especially for TV. Most popular area morning shows, for instance, book their guests six to eight weeks in advance. Don't expect to start with Donahue or Oprah. Big national shows will want to see videos of you in action on local programs before they'll consider you.

There's a knack to deciding whom to approach on a newspaper staff. While the book review editor seems a logical choice, this may not be the ideal place for optimum exposure. Individuals who could use a consumer guide, for instance, aren't typically avid book readers. They would rarely turn to the book review section. You'd be better off approaching the Scene Editor or Living Editor or whatever they call what used to be the "Women's Pages." Likewise, a management title might be more appropriately promoted to the Business Editor—book about horticulture to the Gardening Editor.

Some publishers use a two-step approach and prioritize their media campaign. In the first round they go after the daily papers and major TV and radio shows. Round two gets them in front of the many weekly papers in the area and quite possibly on shows that air at such times as 6:30 A.M. on Sunday morning.

If you've done your job well and have a timely message, they will call you to schedule an interview. What if this doesn't happen and you're missing what you feel is a superior opportunity? Place a discreet phone call to the producer or editor inquiring if they received your media kit. It's amazing how often these materials never get delivered to the proper person or are misplaced.

Radio is a real bonanza for authors. One advantage is you aren't forced to condense your message into three to ten minutes. Instead, you usually have an hour or so to answer questions and elaborate on the merits of your book. (We go into more detail about how to do this in a later chapter.)

It's a good idea to follow up media appearances with a thank-you note. Surprisingly, this is seldom done. Yet it will help you stand out favorably in the reviewer's, interviewer's, or producer's mind.

Radio can also be worked another way. Many stations conduct contests where the third or fifth or fifteenth caller wins an item for guessing something. Does this trigger any ideas for you? How about donating a couple of dozen books to the station in exchange for their giving them out as the prize—and mentioning the title free of charge twenty-four times on the air?

If you do nothing further with the media exposure you receive, however, you're missing an outstanding opportunity. Savvy marketers use the piggyback principle. That means you make copies of written interviews and features by and about you and circulate them. They become another piece in your media kit. Once you have a few electronic interviews under your belt, make a list indicating what shows you've been on. This will reassure other stations they're not dealing with a neophyte who may clam up the second the mike is live. (And ideally, you took a cassette tape along for radio interviews and asked them to tape it for you.) Assuming you did a reasonable job, this gives you a "demo" tape to help convince producers they should book you on even more popular shows. One thing leads to another in the onrushing domino effect of free publicity.

Capturing the Attention of Reviewers

Short of having a professional sales staff capable of selling sand to a sheik, reviews are your foremost sales tools. People put a lot of stock in reviews because they are perceived as impartial third party commentaries. But before you can garner appropriate reviews, you must identify your prime review sources. Earlier we discussed getting complimentary copies to area VIP's. That, however, only scratches the surface.

If you're a self-publisher, even before you have printed books, send galleys or folded and gathered pages. They automatically go to *Publishers Weekly*,

Booklist, Library Journal, Kirkus Reviews, and *Small Press* magazine—plus other appropriate places. Finished books should be sent to the "Source Department" Editor at *American Libraries* and the editor of *Choice*. These are the kingpin reviewers for general trade books. Garnering a review in one or more of these publications will go a long way toward selling out your first print run.

When we put together a nationwide marketing plan for a client, we usually begin by scouring our corporate library copy of *Standard Rate and Data*. This is actually a tool of advertising agencies, but proves especially effective for discovering all sorts of magazines you've probably never heard of. Since it costs several hundred dollars a year to subscribe, use the one at the library. You'll want the editions for "business" and "consumers". By playing detective in these volumes for a few hours you can uncover many solid review possibilities. Other volumes from our corporate reference library that get a lot of use are *The Standard Periodical Directory, National Directory of Magazines,* the *All-in-One Directory, Ulrich's International Periodical Directory, Hudson's Newsletter Directory,* and the *Editor & Publisher Syndicate Directory*.

Now determine what other national newspapers might review your book. You can find major ones listed in *Literary Market Place (LMP)*. Another favorite resource of ours is *Working Press of the Nation,* volume 1, titled "Newspaper Directory". Not only does it list daily and weekly papers for every place in the U.S. with editorial department names, it also catalogs special interest publications. These include college papers, black newspapers, those with a religious bent, and others with a business emphasis. While we're talking about newspapers, don't overlook the alternative press. Most larger U.S. cities sport a weekly alternative or "underground" paper. It could be one of your most ardent supporters if you have a controversial or offbeat subject.

Of course, to the most important of reviewers you'll automatically send a complimentary book (or maybe even galleys), accompanied by promotional literature. Because we operate the Maverick Mail Order Bookstore catalog, we are often on the receiving end of review copies from publishers large and small. What an education! It never ceases to astonish us how many of these books come in with only a packing slip. At a minimum, include a news release with all the pertinent information about your book. For less important reviewers, promo materials along with an offer of the book will probably suffice. While giving away books is cheap promotion, there's no point in throwing them at people who have no intention of giving you any mention.

If you don't crack a vital review source at first, keep in front of it by sending copies of other reviews or comments from respected authorities in your field. Be alert to possible hooks into timely news events or issues. Follow-up is especially important in all areas of promotion. After all, you're competing with many other products for free exposure. So remember that persistence often opens strange—and exciting—doors.

Talk about excitement: Vic Spandaccini about turned flips when he learned *Parade* magazine planned on reviewing his *The Home Owner's Journal* in their "Bright Ideas" column. He had no sense of what to expect. How many of *Parade's* 30,000,000 readers would take the bait? Well, the last time we heard, Vic had received 5,400 orders and they were still coming in at the rate of 30 per week four months later!

This is certainly proof that reviews are one of your chief sales tools. Successful authors and independent publishers aren't just lucky, they're plucky. They are adept at using media promotion and reviews to leverage themselves into positions of power and profit. And they are wise enough to recognize the original review is just the beginning. An even greater advantage awaits those who skillfully reprint, quote, and use that review for future leverage.

Even more power and profit can be yours if you tap into book clubs. We investigate this exciting arena next.

3

Book Club Sales Can Mean Big Bucks

Many small publishers ignore book clubs, feeling they're the domain of major trade houses. Absolutely not true! In fact, we've locked into book club sales that covered all our first-run printing costs. Book club sales do something additional for you: they build credibility. It shows that others in the industry value your work when you can splash across your book cover, or highlight in your promotional materials, the fact you've been selected by a book club. Happily, it isn't necessary to have a fancy, established subsidiary rights department to crack this market. We'll show you how.

Choosing the Right Book Club

Virtually any book published has a potential home with a book club. They come in as many varieties as cookies. Some cater to very broad markets, others to special niches. This segment of publishing is dominated by four powerful entities. Time, Inc. has Book-of-the-Month Club (BOMC is one of the two giants), Quality Paperback Club (QPB), Homestyle Book Club, and some small specific clubs. The other giant, Literary Guild, is owned by Doubleday Book Clubs. They also own niche clubs devoted to theater, mystery, and large print books. Both Better Homes and Gardens Book Clubs and Outdoor Life Book Club also enjoy a strong presence.

Most work on the negative option theory. That means members automatically receive books unless they say no. The large clubs buy for 16 to 18 cycles a year. BOMC buys 20-25 main selections each year. These are very mainstream titles of interest to a broad market. They also place much smaller orders for 8-15 alternate selections.

Dozens of more specialized clubs address individualized interests. There's the Cookery Book Club, Self-Sufficiency Book Club, Aviators Guild, Lawyer's Book Society, Spiritual Book Associates, even the Twenty One Bookclub—which deals in "adult books." And there are over two dozen juvenile clubs for kids as young as two years old.

It's never too early to start thinking of book clubs. Many of the larger ones welcome polished manuscripts. At this infant stage they'll also want to see a mock-up of your cover and be informed about the estimated publication date and price. Additionally, they will need a brief summary of the book, an author biography, and sample illustrations. By working with them early, you give them the option of piggybacking their print run with yours. This has a distinct advantage for *you* since it will slash the unit cost of each book printed. If you're already into the typesetting phase, send them a copy of the galleys.

There is hope even after a title has passed its publication date. QPB and some smaller niche clubs will consider books that aren't brand new. Here's where authors can get involved. Clear it with your publisher, then go after this exciting income opportunity yourself.

It's never too late. Nat Bodian tells of an engineering handbook which had previously been a brisk-selling title. But seven years had passed and sales lagged, so the publisher permitted a book club to reprint 1,000 copies and offer it as an alternate selection. Not only was that a good income generator in itself, but the publisher's sales nearly tripled from the added exposure.

The Book-of-the-Month Club, Inc., receives about 5,000 submissions a year. BOMC has five clubs: Book-of-the-Month Club itself, Quality Paperback Book Club, Cooking & Crafts Club, Fortune Book Club—which handles business books, and the Dolphin Club for sailing enthusiasts. If they're interested in a title, they will offer an advance against royalties for book club rights. This is based on their sales and manufacturing estimates.

Quality Paperback Book Club has, over the last several years, adopted books from over thirty small presses. Offerings from this segment of the publishing community accounted for 12% of their offerings in 1987. "Some of the most interesting writing today is coming from small presses," states Vice President and Managing Director Susan Weinberg.

"QPB members enjoy the unusual, the quality book with a twist that may not find mass market popularity." The club is interested in classic and current works of fiction and nonfiction, including history, reference, biography, science, and humor.

Until recently fifteen different clubs were sheltered under the umbrella of Macmillan Book Clubs, Inc. Titles aimed at teachers, architects, nurses, engineers, and executives—among others—are welcome here. They have further solidified their dominance in the field by purchasing the twelve Prentice Hall Book Clubs from Simon & Schuster. Prentice Hall's special-interest book clubs are aimed at professional markets. The largest ones sell books on the behavioral sciences and general management, while others are targeted at the sales, accounting, personal computer, data processing and educational fields.

Another recent consolidation move concerned Doubleday, which was sold to Bertelsmann, the world's largest marketer of book and record clubs. Within their portfolio is the Literary Guild, Doubleday Book Club, Fireside Theatre, International Collectors Library, Large Print Book Club, Military Book Club, Mystery Guild, and the Science Fiction Book Club.

With the emergence of chain bookstore discounting, book clubs—whose appeal has revolved around offering books at low prices by mail—dare to seek additional ways to be competitive. Doubleday, for instance, plans on stressing elements other than price. The quality of the product will be of more importance. "A club edition could include comprehensive information about the author," comments Peter von Puttkamer, the new CEO of Doubleday clubs. "It could cross-reference to other works by the author, it could contain illustrations by interesting people who have some relationship with the author." von Puttkamer continues, "It becomes a whole different product, a book one can only find in the club."

Bottom Dollar Sense

Just what financial rewards can you expect from such a subsidiary rights sale? That varies widely. It will be influenced by whether your title is a main or alternate selection. Understandably, main selections command more money. With some of the larger clubs, the usual is 10% of the list price, plus extra production expenses to make a club edition. Others will offer an advance against royalties.

When dealing with the smaller specialized clubs, plan on giving about a 70% discount. (Of course, if you've used the proper formulas for pricing your book, this will typically leave you anywhere from a 10 to 20% profit.) Negotiation skills are very important here. Try to get *them* to make a commitment first. Editors usually offer much less than they will settle for. We were initially offered $5.70 per book for one of our client's titles. When the negotiation ended, we had parlayed the price to $8.00 per book.

Some require legal contracts, others just a purchase order. The terms are also negotiable. One club we recently sold to wanted to pay net ninety, but finally agreed to net thirty days when we pushed for more prompt payment. That way, there is cash in hand to pay outstanding printing bills. With some, you can also encourage faster payment by offering a 2% discount for payment within ten days of delivery.

Don't feel the story has ended just because you've made one sale. We sold one client's book to both the Nostalgia Book Club and the Movie/Entertainment Book Club. (They have since merged.) Neither of them required exclusivity. Avoid giving an exclusive on small deals; a second club may come along and want the book later on. (Nat Bodian reports this happened to him—and the second club was BOMC!) While multiple submissions are okay, should you be fortunate enough to peak the interest of more than one of the top four clubs, expect them to demand exclusivity.

Sometimes you can make a second sale to the same club. When we were ready to go back to press for our *National Survey of Newspaper "Op-Ed" Pages*, we alerted Writer's Digest Books, who had previously purchased it for their book club. A day later we had a verbal purchase order for 500 more!

At our book promotion and marketing seminars, the question often comes up, "But won't it cut into my other sales if I let a book club have my book?" Absolutely not. In fact, exposure with a book club creates an "echo effect." People learn about your title through a book club—but they may actually buy it at a bookstore or through your own direct mail promotions. Statistics show that almost half the population has no easy access to a bookstore. So you've nothing to lose and potentially big bucks to gain by exploring the lucrative book club market.

Making Contact

So how do you find out about all these book clubs? There are two ideal sources: *LMP (Literary Market Place)* or *Book Marketing Opportunities: A Directory*. Both publications list dozens of clubs and appropriate contact names. Check for these at your main local library. Both BOMC and Macmillan Book Clubs offer free guidelines. Contact them to obtain a copy. You might also want to call and verify the club editor's name before writing key contacts.

Another potential for profit awaits in the selling of serial and excerpt rights. In the first case, you let a magazine or newspaper dole out your book a little at a time. In the latter, you allow them to extract passages. Read on to discover how this all works.

4

Selling Serial Rights
Without Selling Your Soul

Serial rights sales offer several distinct advantages. First, they give you widespread exposure. When parts of your book are excerpted, or it is condensed in national magazines or newspapers, a huge new base of readers can be stimulated to buy the book. This can also serve to instigate more reviews. In addition, serial rights sales provide a new revenue base, as those publications pay for the privilege of reprinting sections of your work. Canny publishers look for ways to exploit this marketing strategy. If your publisher isn't doing so, ask to have the rights back so you as the author can pursue this avenue.

Serialization sales fall into two categories: first rights and second rights. First rights apply to a forthcoming work and are sold—and typically published—prior to the official publication date. They offer a marvelous way to whet readers' appetites for a title before it ever rolls off the press. Subscribers of the *New Yorker* were so anxious to see the next segment of Truman Capote's *In Cold Blood* they waylaid mail deliveries to get a sneak preview.

First and Foremost Serial Rights

First rights are more lucrative than second. The record high is probably the $200,000 *Woman's Day* shelled out for Rose Kennedy's memoirs. While five-figure sales are not uncommon for major books by well-known authors, this can still be a lucrative field for small presses. It can generate hundreds, often thousands, of dollars in front money—a handy cash reservoir when monthly bills come due. And you needn't be satisfied with just one first rights sale. While publications will normally want exclusivity on the portion they reprint, you can peddle parts of a book to different magazines or newspapers. One book captured *ten* first right serial sales. Sometimes similar material is sold to several magazines with totally different readerships, there being no overlapping competition.

Who are the most promising candidates for first rights sales? The women's magazines are probably the most fertile ground, both for fiction and nonfiction. They gobble up vast amounts of material on such subjects as self-help, beauty, cooking and pop psychology, as well as the standard celebrity titles and novels. *Cosmopolitan*, *Ms.*, *Redbook*, *Good Housekeeping*, *Woman's Day*, *Family Circle*, and *Working Woman* are all prime targets.

For material appealing to the opposite sex, *Playboy* and *Esquire* pay healthy fees. So do tabloids, such as the *National Enquirer*, which is seeking more books for excerpting. The *New York Times Magazine*, the *New York Post*, the *Washington Post*, and other newspapers also serialize books. The list goes on and on. *People*, *Atlantic*, *Reader's Digest*, and such specialized publications as *American Photography*, *Mother*

Jones, Gambling Times, Tennis, and *Parents Magazine* all publish excerpts.

Second Chance Serial Rights

While second serial rights will not generate as much money per sale, they are easier to hawk. Let's face it, there are a lot more publications that can afford a couple of hundred dollars for a piece than there are that can afford thousands. Some magazines, such as *New Woman,* are almost totally made up of serializations. It costs them less to purchase a book excerpt than it does to commission a new article. *Cosmopolitan* is serializing a lot of fiction after the book has come out. If your titles are regional in nature, hone in on area newspapers or regional magazines that target the same audience. Specialty magazines will quite possibly be interested in picking up second serial rights for something relevant to their field. And if you've got an existing book which was never merchandised in this way, it may not be too late if the subject and treatment are still timely.

Finding the Rights Buyers

Precisely how does one go about courting the magazines and newspapers that might be candidates for purchasing rights? The first step is to study your titles. Carefully evaluate parallel subject areas in the magazine industry. Now prospect for specific buyers in *Book Marketing Opportunities: A Directory, LMP,* and *Writer's Market.*

Once you've built a list of likely candidates, prepare a direct-mail package. It could consist of a dynamic introductory sales letter, a news release about the title, and perhaps a mock-up review that shows the scope of the book. Offer to send a complimentary examination copy. When going after important sales, it is also wise to include a sample chapter or two you feel would be particularly appropriate for their audience. Make it *easy* for the editor to see why his or her readers would find this excerpt of interest.

As in all marketing, the secret of success is often follow-up. If you've had no word after a couple of weeks, get on the phone and make sure your package arrived. Have a concise, punchy statement ready. Be sure to share any recent exciting developments, such as a book club sale.

Dotting the I's, Crossing the T's

When you do get an affirmative reply, insist on putting the arrangements in writing. This needn't be a complicated contract; a simple letter stating the details, signed by both parties, does fine. If they are hesitant to prepare one, offer to do it yourself. It should contain the following:

1) What you are selling. (This is usually an excerpt, or a specific portion of the work, for one-time use.)
2) A maximum number of words they are allowed to print.
3) The amount to be paid and when it is due.

4) Timing on the appearance of the material. (If you're selling first rights, be sure the actual appearance of the material in print doesn't hold up your book's publication.)

5) Copyright. (If the magazine is not copyrighted, your excerpt had better be! Some publishers prefer to copyright serializations as a standard procedure.)

Because additional book sales is one of your prime motivations for selling serial rights, it's critical the book be clearly identified. Insist that an "editor's note" appear either at the beginning (preferably) or at the end of the piece. It should state the title of the book, the author, the publisher, and the retail price. Convincing them to include an ordering address is a nice coup.

Whether you're striving to increase book sales— wanting to come to the attention of more reviewers, or needing to give your cash flow a boost—selling serial rights offers a viable road to increased success.

Speaking of success, you'll be delighted at the opportunities available through special sales. The following chapter goes into detail on this exciting way to peddle for profit.

5

Special Sales Equal Lucrative Opportunities

No longer do you as an author have to wail, "My publisher isn't doing anything to sell my book!" Nor should self-publishers be frustrated by the cold shoulder treatment they meet at most bookstores. Why? Because *you* can have a dramatic impact on the sales of your own work! If you've sold your book to a trade publisher, you can usually coordinate with their marketing or publicity manager, feeding ideas and the names of potential sales outlets.

But what if the publisher decides not to pursue your ideas? Then use them yourself to boost sales of your nonfiction title. Put together a plan, share it with the publicity department, and ask them for additional complimentary review copies to help you implement it.

Each year thousands of books are immensely profitable—yet they never see the inside of a bookstore or make "bestseller" lists. They are merchandised by astute people who know how to tap into a potent form of marketing known as "special sales."

This covers everything *outside* traditional retail and wholesale methods.

Our consulting firm, About Books, Inc., has helped clients sell thousands of books. We've gotten titles into doctors' offices, placed them in national catalogs, set up drop-ship arrangements, organized fund-raising promotions, and counseled publishers on how to tap into national grocery store chains.

Don Parker is the author of a book of humorous cop stories called *You're Under Arrest*. He sold 250 copies (non-returnable at a 40% discount) to an Albertson's Food Store. They paid in two weeks, discounted the $14.95 book to $11.95, then placed them at all twelve check out counters. Now we're working with Don to create a ripple effect with Albertson's in other parts of the country.

The Book Industry Study Group released figures in 1988 showing that *one out of every four* books purchased by consumers is bought at a non-bookstore retail outlet. While there are 20,000 bookstores in the U.S., there is probably ten times that number of non-bookstore retail outlets that also sell books. Besides grocery, variety, and drug stores, there are stationery and office suppliers—hobby, toy, and game shops—camera stores—plus gift, souvenir, and tobacco shops. This is not to mention liquor stores —home centers—pet shops—candy stores—computer electronics outlets—auto supply stores—airport shops—convenience outlets—and wholesale club, to name the major options. It is estimated more than 500 million dollars worth of books were sold in this manner in 1987! If you want to cash in on this market, read on.

Outfoxing Bookstores

The secret of special sales success isn't all that profound. It requires a different kind of thinking, however, than most of us are used to. You need to look for ingenious links between your book and other businesses, organizations, and individuals. This matchmaking aligns the product (your book) with those who regularly serve customers interested in the same subject.

How do you find such coalitions? Let's do some brainstorming. Suppose you have a book about gardening. Where would people most likely to need this information be found? How about at nurseries, home improvement centers, garden shops, or garden clubs? A title dealing with glamour, makeup techniques, or dieting will sell at beauty shops. If your book has to do with travel (such as bed and breakfast inns, European customs, or the best area campgrounds), travel agencies or recreational vehicle dealers are prospects. Books on child rearing are naturals for baby shops, day care centers, and toy stores.

A coin dealer might be interested in your book on investing in gold and silver. Repair manuals, home improvement titles, and books about decorating do well in home improvement/handyman-type stores. This is a growing market for books. There are 21,000 of these home centers in the U.S. And if your message appeals to jocks, sporting goods stores should be your target.

By penetrating such specialty outlets, you place your book within easy reach of the ideal customer—many of whom *never* walk into a bookstore. Ron Dornsife, author of *The Ticket Book*—which tells how to talk your way out of a ticket among other tips for motorists—sold over 200,000 copies. One of the innovative places he merchandised his book was in car washes.

Once you've pinpointed companion outlets, it's time to do your homework. Find out what the usual terms of business are in this particular industry. How? Ask; play dumb. Determine what merchandising concepts are compatible with this new channel. Discounts, terms, and conditions must be workable within this industry. Many will want net price information, meaning what is their cost. They are not used to a publisher's typical sliding scale discount. Specialty accounts typically pay within 45 days. Some may even prepay if you offer an additional 2 or 3% discount.

Now orchestrate your approach. Deal with the decision maker: the owner or manager. Personal contact is the most effective method, but telephone sales can also be successful. Be prepared to show why your book will appeal to their customers. Talk in terms of the problems it solves for readers. Explain that carrying it will give them a new revenue base.

You might offer to leave a dozen copies on consignment until the book proves itself. Expect to give a 40 to 50% discount. (The good news is that, unlike bookstores, there are no returns.)

These folks often lack shelf-awareness; fine-tune your sales pitch by providing a complimentary point-of-purchase counter display that will hold several books. Some box companies have ready-made book display cartons. Print a colorful card to attach to the top of the carton to focus attention on your book. Place the display in a high visibility spot, such as on the counter by the cash register. Creating such a merchandising device goes a long way toward assuring you success in these specialty markets.

Pay attention to how the books move. Check back in a week or so and replenish stock. This seems like a lot of work to sell a few books, right? Wrong. You're laying essential groundwork. As soon as you've established a track record at Store A, you can approach Stores B, C, and D—telling of their competitor's success. These sales will be easier than your pioneering one. And once you've got several places in an area selling your book, you're ready to take the Big Step.

To do this, ask one of your accounts who their most effective sales representative is. Contact this person. Tell him or her about all the successful outlets you've established that are within their territory, and suggest they add your book—a proven seller—to their line. Since you've already removed the risk, they'll probably agree. Once that individual is successful, investigate how to contact all the other company reps. Presto! You've just acquired a string of wholesale reps across the country to promote your little ole book!

This concept works in all sorts of environments. One of our clients has a book on nutrition which we've promoted to health professionals. It is now carried by many physicians, dentists, and chiropractors. As retail stores are serviced by sales reps, so is the medical profession. It's simply one step more to learn who calls upon them, make a contact with that wholesaler, and set up a *nationwide chain of distribution*.

Bruce Lansky, who has been outrageously successful in selling books via specialty outlets, also believes in developing a mailing piece for the specialty distributor to use as a statement stuffer when billing accounts. And he publishes a newsletter containing merchandising tips for his specialty accounts. Using these various tactics to sell parenting books in infant stores, Lansky reports this method of distribution accounted for the sale of 100,000 books a month! "That meant there were more copies being sold through infant stores in the Midwest alone than in the entire B. Dalton chain nationwide," he observes.

Establishing Drop-ship Arrangements

While you won't make enough from drop shipments to fund a cruise to the Orient, it's a steady way to sell books. In this type of special sale you set up arrangements with other people—like newsletter editors, for instance—who regularly mail to readers with a parallel interest. To locate these newsletters, check a current edition of *Hudson's Newsletter Directory*, published by the Newsletter Clearinghouse or the *Newsletter Directory*, published by Gale Research Company. Both are cross-referenced by subject category, so finding a group of potential "partners" is easy. There are newsletters that specialize in leisure topics, advertising, health, consumerism, business, retirement, real estate, you name it. Find a common denominator and compose a letter suggesting they advertise your title to their readers in return for keeping a percentage of the retail price.

Here's how it works: They get a cash order, prepare a shipping label, and send you a check for your portion. You mail out the book. It's a win/win

proposition. We set up such an arrangement with
Ad Lib Publication's John Kremer. He sells our
books; we sell his. You may think of others with
whom you can develop a similar program. Someone
with a compatible title might tuck your flyers into
their mailings when they fill book orders. This sales
strategy is called using "bounce backs."

Association Alliances Equal Bulk Sales

Virtually every interest has a national group form-
ed around it. There's the Association of Sports
Museums and Hall of Fame, (got a book on a
sports figure?) or the Underwater Society of Amer-
ica (they might be interested in your treatise on skin
diving). And what about the International Cornish
Bantam Breeders' Association—who could hardly
resist your tome on how to increase poultry yields.
The majority of associations are trade or professional organizations with large memberships and
hefty budgets. To determine which ones are prime
candidates for your work, consult the *Encyclopedia
of Associations* at the library. The association itself
may be interested in buying your book in bulk
quantities. Or they may promote your title to their
membership via reviews and listings in one or more
of their publications.

Do you live in Washington, D.C.? This is the hot
spot for trade association national headquarters.
New York City is next; Chicago runs a close third.
Short of a personal visit to the executive director, a
mailed promotional package, as discussed above, will
do nicely. As in all selling, follow up. Be politely
persistent.

Finding a niche where you have something in common with someone else—being a matchmaker—pays big dividends. Why not seek and exploit some of these exciting special sales opportunities for your book?

There are other ways to move huge amounts of books at one time. The next chapter investigates this strategy.

6

Tapping into
Premium and Incentive Sales

Selling large quantities of your book to a company, organization, or association is an excellent way to boost the bottom line. These are called premium or incentive sales. Books as a segment of the overall premium/incentive market account for a hefty $500 million annually, according to a study done by Time-Life and reported in the February 12, 1988, issue of *Publishers Weekly*. And this way of merchandising shows huge potential, it's growing by 7 to 8% a year.

How Books are Used as Premiums

Books have a "high perceived value" and are used in all sorts of ways. Manufacturers buy them as an incentive for their sales force; corporations purchase them for business gifts. But the largest chunk is sold as consumer incentives, as traffic builders to encourage people to come into a store, or as a reward for a consumer who participates in an offer. They also serve as lower ranking prizes in contests or sweepstakes, as a thank you when one customer refers another, as a gift for listening to a direct selling pitch, or as a premium for spending so many dollars.

Financial institutions have long been heavy users of premiums. They give them for opening a new account, making a substantial deposit to an existing account, taking out a loan, or maintaining a certain balance over a specified period.

Sometimes premiums are considered to be self-liquidating. That means the company buying the books charges recipients a discounted amount that covers the investment put up by the company. Here's an example of how this works: When we spoke with the special sales director at E. P. Dutton, they were in the process of positioning *Winnie the Pooh* with Leaver Brothers. In turn, the food manufacturer plans to offer purchasers of Mrs. Butterworth syrup half price off the book when accompanied by a proof of purchase coupon. Dutton anticipates selling 80,000 copies, yet the consumer will ultimately foot the bill.

No major publisher dominates the field. In fact, many ignore it completely. It's estimated that only one in ten trade houses pursue premium sales. What a wonderful opening for smaller, more aggressive publishers and assertive authors! To capitalize on this situation, let's examine what some of the "biggies" do:

Examples of Trade Publishing Successes

Better Homes and Gardens is one of the most aggressive publishers to exploit this market. They often spin out parts of their larger cookbooks into sixteen-, thirty-two-, or sixty-four-page booklets. Their red plaid cover has high recognition value and is trusted by consumers. For that reason, their premium sales typically start around 50,000 copies — and sometimes run into several million. They also team with manufacturers on complete books. In one especially successful match, Frigidaire bought one of their titles to give to refrigerator purchasers. This giveaway was credited with boosting refrigerators sales by 44%!

St. Martins Press used an innovative twist to sell one of their titles. When they heard the Sylvania nineteen-inch TV had been voted the "best in its field," they convinced Sylvania to buy their book of lists, *The Best of Everything*, as a premium.

Emergency Medical Procedures made a bunch of money for Prentice Hall. Getty Oil asked that the cover be redesigned for them, then bought a large quantity at a 60% discount to be used in auto dealerships and by sales reps.

Graphic Arts Publishing, an Oregon firm, actively merchandises their regional coffee table books. They sell them to banks for VIP customers, to associations for fund raisers, and to JC chapters and state governments for area promotional tools. In one clever move, they sold a book about Maryland to the Maryland Auto Dealers Association.

If you decide to pursue this avenue, remember premium customers swarm around certain areas as bees do around honeycombs. Food and beverage companies are heavy users. In the automotive industry, it's tires, batteries, and accessories. Pharmaceuticals are another possibility. And, of course, banks and savings and loan institutions often present gifts to their customers. Corporate tie-ins are possible as gifts to VIP customers and stockholders, incentives for members of the sales force, or to be used as learning tools.

There are no limitations. *USA for Business Travelers* was a natural for airlines, hotels, credit card companies, and travel agencies. *In Search of Excellence* zoomed to stardom partly because of imposing corporate sales. You're bound only by your own imagination. Bear in mind, however, companies or products favorably mentioned in your book are always prime prospects.

Developing Your Marketing Strategy

There are three primary magazines that can help you expose your book to potential buyers. The granddaddy is *Potentials in Marketing* (50 South Ninth Street, Minneapolis, MN 55402). If they feel your book qualifies, they'll send you a form to fill out. And if you are one of the titles selected, they will run a free plug. They also refer interested people to a reader's service card—a post card where readers are invited to circle certain numbers for more information. The magazine then sends you a computer print out of the names of information requesters. You could get hundreds of requesters for more information. Statistics show about one in ten will typically gel when promptly followed up. If your budget is especially flush—and your title a likely premium candidate—you may even want to run a display ad in this publication.

Other publications that go to those who are your potential customers are *Premium Incentive Business*

(1515 Broadway, New York, NY 10036) and *Incentive Marketing* (633 Third Avenue, New York, NY 10017).

This, however, is but the tip of the iceberg. What about checking trade shows and exhibitions to locate suitable matches? The library has reference books that list such shows all around the country. Perhaps one will be held near you. A few years ago if you had written a book about crock pots or woks, small appliance trade shows would have been a bonanza of potential incentive sales contacts. Ditto for books on computers.

Position yourself with others interested in your market. Think about who else goes to your potential readers—and how your book can serve their needs. Maybe you've identified cereal companies as a target (they're ideal for kids' books). Perhaps it's garden equipment manufacturers or the maker of a well-known beverage.

Now the question is, "How do I find them?" Go to the library and search through *Thomas Register of Manufacturers*. It's a multi-volume set that gives details about virtually every manufacturer in the U. S. Once you find garden equipment manufacturers, for instance, make a list. Always include the name of a primary contact person. We suggest the vice president of sales, but titles vary. He or she may be called the "director of marketing," or something similar.

Put together a dynamic sales letter plus other information about your book and how it will meet their needs. Include a complimentary copy. These are busy corporate executives. After a couple of weeks, get on the phone and follow up with a polite call to inquire if they received your package.

The Mechanics of How It All Works

Don't expect anything to happen fast. One of the drawbacks of premium/incentive sales is that they take a long time to develop—usually months, sometimes up to a year. For that reason, this may be a strategy you decide to employ after you already have books in print. But these sales are worth waiting for! Most fall in the range of from 5,000 to 100,000 copies. They'll probably want to buy a couple of hundred for initial testing purposes before they commit to a large quantity.

Be flexible. Some premium purchasers will want to customize the cover to include their name. (Allow for this extra expense when putting together your deal.) They may buy all—or a part—of your book. They may want slight modifications to the text, or to add something to make it more appealing to their customers. And now to the $64,000 question: What do you charge? Whatever the traffic will bear, of course. Most premium sales on smaller amounts range from 50 to 70% off the retail price. In large volume, experienced buyers will expect to pay manufacturing costs plus 10%. Be sure to get a written purchase order or agreement that spells out details, such as who pays the freight. If there is any question about the integrity or financial status of the company with which you're dealing, insist on at least half payment before you go to press, or establish an escrow account to hold the money.

When we discuss this topic in our seminars, attendees often ask if they can sell to more than one company. The answer is a qualified "yes." Your customers have the right to expect exclusivity—either within their industry or their geographical area. You don't sell to one market chain, for instance, then go to their nearby competitor and try to strike a deal. If you sell a book on household hints to a washing machine manufacturer, steer clear of similar manufacturers.

Books are popular premiums. They rank above such items as cameras, toys, calculators, and luggage. People don't usually throw a book away. It has lasting value. Merchandising yours as a premium or incentive will give you lasting value as well.

You're not so shy you hang your head, dig your toes into the ground, and wring your hands when facing an audience are you? If not, there's another viable way to vend books.

7

Speaking as a Vehicle to Merchandise Books

Tapping into the presentation market—which includes seminars, workshops, lectures, demonstrations, and readings—can open lucrative doors for additional book sales. In fact, Chicago author Bill Joseph earned more than $2 million during a five year period from seminar fees. That was much more than the book itself generated. Yet his book was the key to getting students to attend the seminars.

Before Tom Peters gained fame as an author, he was earning $42,500 a year. Now he gets nearly that for a single day's speaking engagement! His fee is a whopping $30,000 per appearance. Peters has cut back to 125 a year and is already booked into 1991. While these gentlemen are the exceptions, there can be big bucks in what is known in the trade as "back-of-the-room sales."

Developing Back-of-the-Room Sales

Some entrepreneurial authors not only peddle their own books, but put together packages of additional compatible materials. These are then combined, shrink wrapped, and offered at special discounts to seminar attendees. This is grand slam bookselling. And the approach also works well for a publishing house with several titles in the same genre. A charismatic author/speaker could not only promote his or her own books, but other titles as well.

As oregano gives added zest to spaghetti sauce, you can give book sales new zip by exploring this avenue. Lectures or seminars work well for nonfiction; demonstrations are excellent for cook books, new diet regimes, and certain how-to topics. Readings are the most suitable vehicle to highlight poetry and selected fiction. You have a captive audience who, when properly primed, are eager to buy.

It's always easier if you can find an organization or business to sponsor your presentation. Perhaps the "friends of the library" or a local bookstore features poetry readings and excerpts from novels. A gourmet shop or health food store is a natural for food demonstrations. Extended studies or adult education facilities often sponsor one or two day seminars on a wide range of subjects. When Marilyn wrote *Creative Loafing*, she convinced a San Diego recreational association and a savings and loan to sponsor seminars on "Creative Loafing." We sold lots of books to the folks who attended those events.

If your aim is book sales rather than personal glory, choose the places where you appear carefully. While authors with a flair for the spoken word can volunteer as guest speakers at business, professional, civic, or social groups, this quickly becomes a time gobbler with minimal results. It's hard to sell a general interest book to a general interest audience. A title on collecting foreign coins won't stimulate a general audience; but get yourself invited to address a group of numismatics and watch sales zoom.

Launching Your Own Seminar Program

Should you decide to launch your own seminar program, be prepared to work hard. Advertising and promotion are crucial. How will you attract attendees? Will you use a direct marketing campaign? Newspaper space advertising? Radio spots? A referral fee arrangement? News releases to key media?

How much must you charge to make a profit? When and where will the seminars be held? How will attendees register or get information? Who will handle book sales? Overseeing all the details can be as heart-stopping as walking into a microwave cook off wearing a pacemaker.

Besides a lot of work, self-sponsored seminars can be expensive. Suppose you plan on doing a mailing to 5,000 people. Have any idea what that will run? You'd better! To rent the list you'll probably pay around $350. Prices to print a direct marketing package vary greatly. You might get by with about $900; more likely you'll spend double that. (And we're assuming here you write the promotional copy yourself. Many people elect to hire a seasoned professional for this crucial step.) Then there are the costs of a fulfillment house to physically do the mailing. This tacks a few more cents onto every piece. Bulk mail for this size list will typically be 16.7 cents each. It doesn't take a mathematical genius to deduct that you'd better have a lot of people at a reasonable price—or a few people at a high price—to make any money.

Honing Your Presentation Style

Your actual presentation style has a lot of bearing on how book sales go. If you're a dynamic, animated speaker people are much more likely to want to take home a memento of the occasion—your book. Friendliness and a smile go a long way in winning over an audience. Make people feel welcome and comfortable and they'll likely be on your side.

A recent study revealed that 55% of the audience responds to your body language and facial expression, while 37% react to your voice—including pacing, pitch, inflections, and overall delivery. Only 8% react to the actual content of your message! Based on these findings, the more showmanship you have, the more you'll sell. Be sure to hold up your book and mention the title at least twice during the talk.

There are many little tricks for making your presentation successful. First, be sure to take along an adequate supply of books. Sounds simple, right? Yet many authors deliver a compelling speech, rouse their audience to action, then have to turn away sales because they don't have enough stock on hand to meet the demand. What a waste. Also take along customer brochures and leave them in a conspicuous place. Sometimes people won't purchase now, but might later if they have ordering information handy. Or they might want to pass along information to a friend or colleague who may be interested in your title.

Another key strategy is to make it easy to buy. If you plan to use this method of merchandising extensively, arrange with a local banker to offer Visa and MasterCard. And get some desk-type display signs to announce you accept credit cards. It is wise to charge a round number like $7 or $10 or $20, rather than $7.30 or $9.88 or $19.65. That way customers aren't bothered fishing for change to pay sales tax and you aren't tied up over pennies while those who want to spend dollars wait unattended. You can afford to absorb the tax anyway as these sales are usually at full retail price.

Most professional speakers coach the person who introduces them. Many go so far as to provide a typed, double spaced "canned" introduction. That way, there is no temptation for the introducer to say something like, "Jim really needs no introduction." Every presenter needs—and deserves—a well-rounded introduction to establish his or her credentials and set the stage properly. Professionals also ask the person introducing them to wrap up the presentation with "You can get your personally autographed copy of Jim's new book by stopping to see him now at the table in the back of the room." This reminder is often the clincher.

Sources for More Exposure and Information

If lecturing and seminar-giving figure prominently in your plans, it might be worth considering two additional things. The American Society of Association Executives puts out an annual *Association Speakers Directory*. Listings include name, address, phone, and a short description of the topics addressed by each speaker. There is a fee to be listed, but it could prove inexpensive advertising for a subject of interest to this professionally-oriented audience. The ASAE is located at 1575 Eye Street, N.W., Washington, DC 20005.

Another source we highly recommend is the National Speakers Association. (Members of NSA are listed in a directory, receive a newsletter of insider tips, can gain tremendous insights at the annual convention and regional workshops, and have the option of joining area chapters for networking, support, and promotion within the area.) The fellow members we know in NSA are a uniquely caring group of folks. For information write 3877 North 7th Street, Suite 350, Phoenix, AZ 85014, or call 602-265-1001.

Are you an East Coast poet or novelist? Then Poets & Writers, Inc. might sponsor a reading or workshop program in the state of New York. In one year, they doled out over $200,000 to authors. Presentations are given at libraries, "Y's," community centers, small presses, universities, museums, hospitals, prisons, bookstores, and religious facilities. Reach Poets and Writers, Inc., at 72 Spring Street, New York, NY 10012.

Of course, not every book lends itself to merchandising in the ways we've been discussing. And certainly not every author feels comfortable in front of an audience. In many cases, though, employing "back-of-the-room" sales have netted "front-of-the-line" profits.

Even the best book needs written literature to convince prospects to buy it. Do you have an effective customer brochure? If not, read on....

8

Creating a Compelling Consumer Brochure

Virtually every product or service needs promotional literature to convince potential buyers of its merits. A book is no exception. Publishing companies with several titles typically put out catalogs, which have brief descriptions about each of their books. This works well for the trade: bookstores, wholesalers, and libraries. But what about reaching consumers direct? How are they to know about the benefits of a specific book unless you've developed a brochure or flier devoted exclusively to that title?

It quickly becomes obvious that authors and small publishers require some device to promote a single book to a single customer. Shouldn't you learn how to develop a brochure that stands out from the pack? You'll use this piece of literature in a multitude of ways. It's a fast and effective way to respond to daily inquiries from potential book buyers. You can hand it to prospective customers whom you meet in person. It makes an ideal direct mail piece to use when prospecting for sales. Or you can routinely stuff one in packages and letters you mail.

And it can be placed on tables at trade shows, book fairs, and networking meetings.

Your brochure has an additional function. One that is well crafted also serves a peripheral PR purpose. Attach a copy of it to other paperwork when talking to your banker—if you consult in the book's subject area, include it with proposals—and share it with potential employees.

Initial Planning Decisions

A good plan is to a book promoter what a scalpel is to a surgeon—not a substitute for skill, but a tool to increase success. Think about how you intend to use your brochure. Will it be to promote an existing book? To announce a new one? To impress someone? Will you provide a quantity to other authors or publishers who distribute your book? If so, leaving a place for them to customize it with their own ordering information can be a smart move. Is there an advantage to coding or folding some differently from others? Who is your target audience? What are their likes and dislikes? Of course, it never hurts to study the competition. Make a collection of other book promotion pieces. Learn from what they do well—and note things to avoid.

We're not talking about thousands of dollars to create a brochure. You needn't be that ambitious. While four-color photographs reproduced on glossy paper and cut into unusual shapes makes for an impressive piece, this isn't necessary. There is a happy medium between that extreme and plain black ink on cheap white paper. It is important you project a quality image. Your brochure is your sales-person.

Think of an 8 1/2 x 11 inch or 8 1/2 x 14 inch (legal size) piece of paper, printed on both sides and folded to fit into a normal #10 business en-velope. This is an ideal size as it easily slips into a man's inside jacket pocket or a woman's handbag. Folding the paper creates six or eight (depending on which size of paper you use) surfaces. Let's call each of these a panel. Now that we've determined the size of our brochure, it's time to consider what it will contain.

Including the Right Components

Just as a loaf of bread needs flour, liquid, yeast, and other ingredients, a successful brochure needs standard elements. Form follows function. Conclude what the contents should be first, then think about design. If you try it the other way around, you'll feel like you've been caught in a thunderstorm with a leaky umbrella. The design should grow logically out of the subject matter. We'll be talking more about design later.

First, you must grab the potential buyer's atten-tion. This is usually done with a headline and an eye-catching graphic on the front panel. Its sole purpose is to lure the reader into the brochure. Next you have introductory copy that describes your book and addresses the specific needs of your pros-pects.

Include an author biography. Tell why you're qualified to write the book; mention appropriate affiliations that contribute to your credibility. And

include a photograph. People like to see what the person they are dealing with looks like. You can use either a "head shot," which is the typical canned photograph, or an action photo of you doing something. Photos often need editing just like manuscripts. In this case, it takes the form of cropping. Delete extraneous things and focus on the author to achieve the desired effect. Photo captions are a good place to emphasize key benefits. They are one of the most read parts of a brochure.

And while we're talking of photographs, by all means include one of the book—ideally angled to show the spine so people can see it's the real thing. If you're still in the cover design stage, a sharp thumbnail sketch from your graphic designer will suffice to give a reasonable portrayal of the book. When doing other brochure photographic work, suggest the photographer add a new perspective by changing his or her point of view. Shoot down from a ladder or up from floor level. This will add freshness to your photographic images.

Of course, impartial third party endorsements are a key element. Testimonials in the form of advance comments or reviews inject clout into your overall message. Try to get a diversity of comments. Think about your target audience and include quotes that will appeal to different niches of potential buyers.

Include a money-back guarantee. (Notice the boxed "Absolutely No Risk Guarantee" included in the visual.) Give your prospective customers every reason to trust you. After all, you're expecting them to send you money for something they've never seen or handled. Guarantees are sales stimulators. If you're offering a quality product, returns will be a tiny fraction of your sales.

Ask for the order. Just as a good speech has an introduction, body, and conclusion, so does a brochure. You must close the sale. Tell readers what you want them to do—call your toll-free 800 number or send in the order coupon. You can create a sense of urgency by encouraging them to act "today" or "right away."

Be sure to include an order coupon. It can be attached, such as in the adjacent visual, or done as a separate form. But don't overlook a reply device; tests prove coupons multiply responses. It's also a good idea to include ordering information in small print somewhere else on the brochure. That way if it is detached from the order coupon, people can still reach you.

Your company name should appear several times. Notice in the sample for our revised paperback edition of *The Complete Guide to Self-Publishing*, "Communication Creativity" appears not only on the return address logo, but in three other places. If your brochure is designed as a self-mailer, naturally an outer panel must be devoted to the address section.

Sales Sizzle: Express Benefits Over Features

There are a few individuals on this earth who could sell sand to a sheik, but most of us have to work at being strong salespeople. You'll seduce prospects much faster with a "you" approach rather than "me" or "we" or "I." All of us like personalized copy that addresses our needs. Don't just describe your product; tell prospective customers what the product will do for them. When you emphasize benefits instead of features, you tell the customer what he or she will derive from the book—you give tangible reasons to buy. And you slant the essence of your book, its special mystique, towards solving consumer's problems.

Let's look at an example of how to do this: suppose you have a book on entertaining. Instead of listing what goes into planning a dinner party, tell prospective readers their dinner party will be a smashing success. That's the result they want. If your title is about memory improvement, point out that these techniques will have them astounding their friends and impressing their business associates. And they'll never need to be embarrassed again because they've forgotten someone's name.

Got a book on inventory control? Don't preach about how you'll set up and monitor their inventory control system. Instead tell them inventory shortages and surpluses will be a thing of the past. Maybe your title is about physical fitness. People don't want to hear about diet and exercise. Instead romance them by explaining how they—and their friends—will see a marked improvement in their appearance and stamina.

To arouse a potential buyer, use punchy verbs and adjectives. That doesn't mean totally unleash your imagination. Terms like "miraculous," "magic," or "spectacular" sound unconvincing and exaggerated. On the other hand, words with honest pizzazz produce the greatest positive mood change. Cut through the communications chatter with clear, memorable copy that offers prospects instant solutions to nagging problems.

There are three types of brochure readers. The causal reader spends a few seconds scanning the headline on the front panel. The interested reader opens your brochure and reads the headlines, but nothing more. The serious reader devours everything. Your aim is to convert casual readers to interested readers, then to serious readers. What this tells is we'd better concentrate our energies on headlines and sub-heads. They are the carrots dangling before prospective book buyers.

Be aware of what we call "information shaping." How one presents information—what isn't said as much as what is—can prove a creative way to present your story. You can mold information to suit your own purposes. Take, for instance, the two teams that played against each other. It is easy enough for the winner to say "we won!" But a clever loser might comment, "We came in second and the other team came in next to last." Statistics are constantly "shaped" when they are taken out of context. Occasionally, reviews also suffer from similar tampering.

One last thought about writing copy. Avoid terminology or information that "dates" your brochure. Rather than saying the book has been in print for five years, say since 1984. If you must include information that will soon change, consider putting it on a single sheet which will fit into the regular brochure. It will be much cheaper to produce than redoing the whole brochure. And watch photographs so they don't show faddish clothes or other tip-offs that will make your brochure obsolete.

Designing for "Aye" Appeal

Graphic design is the body language of a brochure. As you grapple with this issue, there are several questions to answer. What tone will you set? Friendly? Elegant? Humorous? Professional? Avant garde? Decide on the feeling you want to convey. Of course, this is not exclusively the domain of design. Copy must work with graphics to establish a harmonious whole.

Unlike ads, which tell your story on one flat surface, a brochure allows the reader to see only the front panel initially. Your headline must seize attention. Be pithy and benefit-oriented. Generate interest. The adjacent photo or graphic should actively support and correlate with the headline. Together they make a forceful statement to woo readers inside.

One trick for giving your overall brochure variety and focusing attention on key points is to use "call out" boxes. These are frequently employed in magazine articles where editors extract a sentence or two from the text and run it in larger type. This gives you another shot at interested readers. If the headlines don't catch their fancy, perhaps your call out boxes will.

For visual diversity, there are other options besides photographs. Illustrations can be tailored to your needs and add zest to an otherwise dull brochure. If you can't afford to hire an artist, there's always clip art. Check at an artist supply store for information on what's available.

When you're planning how to put the various elements together, give special consideration to the order coupon. Notice how ours is on an end panel and facing out for writing convenience. It's easily clipped and doesn't destroy the rest of the brochure when removed. This also gives you greater flexibility. Need a brochure for more institutional purposes—such as a mailing to libraries, bookstores, or wholesalers? Simply cut off the order coupon and you have it!

If you're using a self-mailer approach, plan your address panel back-to-back with the order coupon—especially if you do a lot of direct mail campaigns. That way when people return the coupon, you have the coding on their address label on the back and can track which mailing list is pulling best.

Also consider what you want on the address panel if you're heavily into direct mail. Do you need a bulk mail permit number? Should you be printing FORWARDING AND ADDRESS CORRECTION REQUESTED to clean your mailing list? It's a good idea to check with the post office to make sure what you're planning satisfies all postal regulations.

Let's talk a moment about type. Type faces come in different personalities. Some are casual, some formal, some sophisticated, some just plain fun. Unless you're going for a specific effect, stick to standard type faces. And don't mix several different styles. The most you want is one face for the text and another for headlines.

Did you know all-capitalized words are difficult to read—not to mention less pleasing? In fact, lower-case text is read 13.4% faster than copy set in all caps. So be wary of putting many headlines in all caps. You can have the right-hand margins justified (meaning all the same length) or kept ragged right. The latter gives an open feeling as there is more white space.

A reminder when using your logo: work from an original, if possible, rather than taking one off a business card or letterhead. This sacrifices sharpness.

Also consider how the brochure will fold. There are several options. Most good books on printing show samples. Just be sure to avoid unusual sizes that require a customized envelope. This drives costs through the roof. Also special cut outs, called die cuts, cost mucho dinero. If you let a designer talk you into either of these, you'll feel as unlucky as the person who moved into a new town...and was run over by the welcome wagon.

Cost-Effective Production Tips

Perhaps the best advice we can give you here is to proofread carefully. Then do it again! Nothing is more aggravating—and costly—than getting 5,000 brochures from the printer only to discover a glaring error. Mistakes at this point are as unwelcome as ants at a picnic. In addition to diligently proofing regular text copy, carefully examine addresses and phone numbers, the spelling of reviewers' names, and headlines. Double check every detail. Get someone else to inspect things, too; one person can repeatedly overlook the same error.   Two colors of ink are preferred, but even one color used imaginatively will do the trick for the budget conscious. Please don't settle for plain black ink. Going to a color only adds about $15 and will energize your literature. Look at PMS color swatches at an artist supply store or your printers. There's no need to settle for the standard blue, red, green, etc. By the way, studies show younger people prefer bright hues, while older folks respond to soft colors.

To get more mileage out of ink, talk to your designer about using screens of 20 or 30%. This lays down a lighter shade of the color over which you can print text in the full strength ink color. Of course, with a cookbook or travel title, a color photograph of the book is a real plus. If you do use one, in addition to boosting the actual printing price, you'll also need to have a color separation done.

While we're discussing color, there's another option for variation. How about using a colored paper stock? (Just be sure to take into consideration what will happen when you add the ink color. If you were to use a yellow paper with blue ink, for instance, you'd end up with green!)

Nowadays, paper is a large part of the expense of any printing job. Consult with your printer to see if he or she stocks a paper in quantity that will work for you. Coated stocks that appear glossy will cost more, but add an elegant look. They come in various weights. Beware of one too flimsy as its lack of substance will downgrade the feel of your brochure.

Get a written price quotation (not an estimate) from several printers. You may be surprised at the wide variance in charges. Be sure you think through your project first and determine what the bid should include. What quantity? Most people print at least a years projected supply. How many folds? Are half-tones needed for photographs? Any trims? Bleeds? What is their turnaround time? If they say 21 days, they mean over four *working weeks*, not three calendar weeks. Encourage your print rep to make suggestions for cost cutting measures. And when the job is done, we recommend you get the camera-ready art back. Then there's no question about who has it if you need to make changes before going back to press.

A compelling brochure is a sure-fire way to cultivate consumer purchases—and help you get back to press faster on your book! Without one, you resemble a turtle in a horse race. These tips will enable you to get swiftly out of the starting gate and create winning sales literature to promote and sell more books.

Maybe you're looking for a way to tailor your writing to subjects closer to home. Or perhaps you believe in capitalizing on trends. In either case, we next explore how to do just that.

9

Regional Publishing Can Pay Big Dividends

Independent publishers and authors are discovering they can often capture increased profits—with fewer headaches—by focusing on regionally oriented titles. These books range from area Who's Who directories and Yellow Pages to tourist, activity, and consumer guides. The recent spate of city and regional books also includes cookbooks, historical works, nature field guides, and lavish coffee-table books. We became aware of the trend about a year ago when more and more of the client inquiries coming into our consulting firm were concerned with this field of specialty publishing.

There are sound reasons for the current popularity of this genre of publishing. First, it is markedly easier to merchandise a book in a limited geographical region than it is to market it nationwide. You know the area, have ready access to it, and can work it effectively—rather than being at the mercy of book stores and wholesalers thousands of miles away. Virtually every book store has a section for area titles. This is especially important to the one-book self-publisher, who has an enormous problem getting shelf space across the country.

Second, the availability of desktop publishing has attracted many entrepreneurial types to our industry. They are quick to recognize various forms of directory publishing lend themselves ideally to selling advertising or listings within a book. Thus, income opportunity can be milked from two distinct approaches.

Third, as Americans who once vacationed abroad come to fear potential terrorist activities, they now travel more in the U.S. Lower gasoline prices have also given a boost to domestic travel. It's a simple case of supply and demand. These circumstances have created a fresh call for area travel guides.

Like all publishing, you must start with a viable product if you hope to reap financial rewards. A key question is will your area support a title? You can anticipate selling between 500 and 1,500 copies per 100,000 population. Consider, too, many communities swell to more than double their normal size during the tourist season. This can have a spectacular impact on financial projections if your title is tourist oriented.

If all systems are "go" at this point, it's time for market research to find your special niche. Fortunately, you don't need megabucks to conduct the kind of market research multimillion dollar companies indulge in. Your research will be much less sophisticated and, in most cases, free. Just because it doesn't cost a lot, don't underestimate its importance. Choosing your subject wisely is paramount. Savvy publishers don't simply get a bright idea, then rush out and print 5,000 books.

You may not even know at this point what kind
of book you want to publish, only that it appears to
be a sound business move. In which case, you're
searching for a topic that hasn't been done—casting
about for a need to fill. The options are many.
Sometimes good ideas can be obtained by talking to
local librarians or booksellers.

Prospecting for an Appropriate Subject

Domestic travel has mushroomed. As people travel
more in the U.S. they create a demand for guide
books. They need restaurant guides—information
about popular local attractions—books revealing out-
of-the-way intrigues—activity guides for hikers,
skiers, golfers, rafters, and every imaginable pastime.
(According to *Publishers Weekly*, book store personnel say these "participation" books are one of the
hottest categories on the shelves.) A slightly different twist is the nature field guide. It deals with
the flora and fauna of a region. If you're an out-
doors person, perhaps area animals, birds, wild
edibles, trees, or wildflowers would tap your expertise and make an interesting book.

Consumer guides are another good bet because
they're "cross over" books. Not only do they appeal
to local residents, they're also gobbled up by travelers. These guides are usually designed to help you
save money and shop more efficiently. Victoria and
Glen Reed published *Best Buys in San Francisco*. It
reveals such secrets as how to save 20% off books,
where to get brand name cosmetics at 70% off, and
even gives a source for buying famous label mens-
wear at a 60% discount. If you know where to find

bargains in your vicinity, and no good book exists on the subject, this is an opportunity waiting to be capitalized on.

Special interest books are another possibility. They address the particular curiosities of certain segments of the population. Some real life examples are the *Children's Guide to Santa Fe, Single in Portland: Living Fully on Your Own, The Seattle Actor's Handbook, Alabama Showdown: the Football Rivalry Between Auburn and Alabama,* and (ahem) *The Traveler's Guide to the Best Cat Houses in Nevada.* As you can see, with special interest books, there is something for e-v-e-r-y-o-n-e.

Some publishers are doing nicely by spinning out legal tomes that relate to their particular state. As noted in a previous issue of *Small Press,* Nolo Press began in 1971 with a little book called *How to Do Your Own Divorce in California.* That was the initiation of a publishing enterprise that today does more than a million dollars a year in business and has some fifty titles in print. They have virtually cornered the market in California with various books on divorce, eviction, and incorporation. Texas is another state with a strong emphasis on legal books. There is *Texas Probate, How to Incorporate Your Texas Business,* and *Texas Law in Layman's Language.*

Are you a history buff? Do you live in a community rich in historical fact and fancy? History books wear as many costumes as Halloween trick-or-treaters. There are books on railroad lore, such as Dick Murdock's *Smoke in the Canyon: My Steam Days in Dunsmuir* (which sold over $600 worth in one day). Then there are political Odysseys like *Pioneers and Politicians,* which profiles ten Colorado governors—beginning in the territory days. Architecture sometimes provides the impetus for a historical book. A case in point is *Last of the Handmade Buildings: Glazed Terra Cotta in Downtown Portland.* Folklore and ghost towns are more popular historical themes.

Cookbooks centering around a specific region are typically steady sellers. This is partially because some people collect cookbooks like others collect sea shells or matchbook covers. Women's organizations have had phenomenal success producing area cookbooks. The Lafayette Junior League is approaching sales of 450,000 on their *Talk About Good.* The Baton Rouge Junior League rakes in profits of from $100,000 to $150,000 every year from their two cookbooks. This may be a fertile field for a nonprofit organization to which you belong.

Directory publishing is especially appealing to those whose veins pulse with entrepreneurial blood. Many are putting themselves in the black by publishing Yellow Pages. When AT&T was forced to divest itself in 1984 this opened the door for a flood of privately owned area telephone directories.

According to Wall Street analysts, directories cost little to produce and yield a profit margin of up to 20%! The advertising revenue generated by such a book has put many a publisher on easy street. Fred N. Grayson created the Family Pages and targets the Manhattan area. He projected a gross of $200,000 the first year. A new twist is to "position" your book by addressing the needs of a certain segment of the population. Today we know of directories that target senior citizens (the Silver Pages), ethnic communities, and specific industries.

Who's Who Directories are especially popular vehicles since they carry hefty price tags and are frequently bought by the individuals listed in them. And many Who's Who publishers also have additional gimmicks. They offer plaques or certificates for sale to those who are profiled.

Another idea for a lucrative annual publication is media guides which list the newspapers, magazines, radio, and TV sources in a given area. These are high-priced volumes that are sold to advertising and PR firms, government agencies, and corporations doing research on a geographic location. In our guide on the subject, *How to Make Big Profits Publishing City and Regional Books*, we even tell of a media directory publisher who has succeeded in franchising his idea all across the country! See ordering information for this title in the back of this book.

With many Americans sidestepping travel abroad in favor of seeing more of the U.S., area travel guides are red hot these days. Some of them focus on typical tourist attractions, others on little-known haunts, still others take the form of restaurant guides. The numbers here can be impressive. Sasquatch Books has sold over 95,000 copies of their *Northwest Best Places*. Ulysses Press has over 70,000 copies in print of their bestselling *Hidden Hawaii*— and they've gone on to publish a whole series of hidden books. Lance Tapley has 50,000 copies in print of his *Uncensored Guide to Maine*.

A recent article in *Publishers Weekly* noted that book stores have had especially brisk sales in "participation" books. A close cousin to regular guide books, these activity guides cover such subjects as hiking, golfing, scuba diving, white water rafting, skiing, etc. A few cases in point include *New York in Twelve Easy Walks*, *Rock Hunting in Texas*, *The*

Hiker's Guide to Colorado, and *Fishing in Northern California*.

Regional publications branch into remarkable directions. There are trivia books, literary collections, corporate biographies, even maps that put grins on their creator's faces all the way to the bank. Now suppose you have an idea of what you'd like to do. What's next?

Checking Out the Competition

For those who already have an idea, the first step is to learn about your competition. It's surprising how many prospective clients come to us with a tale of woe. They've already published a book—only to discover *afterwards* another existing book covers the subject very nicely. The moral of the story is to do your homework. Know about any competing titles! Then you're able to make an informed judgement if you should proceed, and how to make your book better.

Major bookstores in the area are good places to start. Scour the shelves on area titles; talk to the manager and buyers about your idea. Get their feedback. Did a similar title flop in the past? Could they speculate why? Just because something wasn't successful before, doesn't mean yours won't be. The previous book could have suffered for several reasons. Maybe it was shoddy looking, disorganized, or incomplete.

The visitor and convention bureau (V&CB)—or the local chamber of commerce if you don't have a V&CB—is an excellent place to prospect for information. Make an appointment to see the executive director. He or she will probably refer you to a subordinate. By starting at the top, however, you're more likely to be directed to the person who will have the needed information. For any kind of a tourist activity, or historical guide, the V&CB is an ideal early research point. They not only know what other books might be in print, they have racks overflowing with promotional brochures and booklets containing wonderful information from which you can sift ideas for your own book.

The main library might be your next stop. Look in the card catalog subject index to guide you to the appropriate section. After you've perused the books there, seek the acquisition librarian who is responsible for buying regional titles. Share your idea. Once again, ask for professional feedback.

Now track down the most current edition of *Books in Print*. While area books are not listed as a separate category, with a little sleuthing you can usually uncover the required information. Check your city name in the Subject and Title volumes to determine if other books are available on a related topic. Additionally look under "guide," "cookbooks," "directory," "history," or other key words appropriate to your book. (Keep your eyes open in general when you're scanning *BIP*. We've unearthed many a clever title twist or promo phrase there that lent itself to being adapted to our own use.) Before leaving this research phase, also check in *Forthcoming Books in Print*. Here your detective work will reveal any books soon to roll off the presses.

While you're at the library why not spend a little time studying the volumes on the shelves? What do you think of their covers? Are the interiors of the books designed well? Do they contain editorial

material that could be reslanted for your book to
make it more useful? Is the data presented in a
logical, well organized manner? Are maps or other
visuals placed where they are easy to use? Have
helpful checklists been included? Before you leave,
examine the vertical files. Libraries collect brochures
and pamphlets on a wide range of subjects. You
could find a mother lode of information waiting
here to be mined.

Suppose you discover there is already a good
book covering what you'd hoped to write about. Is
all lost? Not necessarily. Perhaps you can "position"
your book differently.

Positioning Your Book for Stronger Sales

Let's say you wanted to do a restaurant guide to
Boston, but there already is one. How about taking
a more specific, targeted approach? You might do a
book on eating out with kids in Boston, or a vege-
tarian's guide to dining and health food shopping in
Boston. Another option is a guide to historic eater-
ies in Boston.

If there is already a general guide to your city,
how about developing one slanted for children? Or
seniors? Or gays? Or singles? While there are
oodles of guide books to San Francisco, there was
still room for *San Francisco by Cable Car* because it
took a unique approach to seeing the city. And *The
Great Chefs of San Francisco* separated itself from
all the other restaurant guides to this enchanted
land by profiling thirteen of the masters. (This
presented a shrewd marketing angle as well. Thous-

ands of copies were sold by the thirteen restaurants whose chefs were featured.)

Inns With Ocean Views carved its own niche in the bed and breakfast directory market, appealing to vacationers who love the sea. KiKi Canniff's *Oregon Free* and *Washington Free* are as handy for budget-conscious tourists as pockets are on a shirt.

Each of these books appeals to a specific segment of the overall tourist population. That's their secret for success. By positioning your product in this way, you can give yourself a distinct sales advantage and more easily reach your target market.

Circumstances sometimes open new horizons, too. For instance, Canada's Expo 86 drew unprecedented numbers of visitors to Vancouver during its six-month run. Many northwest publishers capitalized on the influx of tourists by coming out with books. While these extra titles would have glutted the market under normal circumstances, most of them were quickly snatched up by Expo attendees.

Opportunities abound when a city or state celebrates important anniversaries. This always prompts extra publicity which, in turn, stimulates tourism. Texas's Sesquicentennial gave rise to a raft of special books about the state and its inhabitants. We even helped tiny Monte Vista, Colorado, develop a book called *Bridge to Yesterday* to celebrate their Bicentennial. When did your state join the Union or your city become incorporated? Is an important anniversary looming on the horizon? Why not put out a regionally oriented book to capitalize on the influx of people and capture part of the spotlight (and the revenue) yourself?

Selling Strategies for Regional Titles

The local press, radio, and TV is more likely to give you key exposure when the book focuses on the community and the author is a resident. Radio talk shows have a voracious appetite. They are a perfect place to promote your book. They'll gobble up a topic that deals with local consumer, activity, or tourist information.

It is also feasible to create an "event" that ties in with the book's theme and will draw media attention. Remember the success story we discussed in Chapter 2 when Foghorn Press did this in spades for their first title, *Forty Niners, Looking Back*.

Another shrewd way to merchandise titles is to put together premium deals. Area businesses and associations are often receptive to sponsoring a book. Merchants such as hotels, banks, car rental agencies, sporting goods outlets, department stores, and insurance companies give away books as a good will gesture to encourage business. Sometimes corporations purchase copies for their employees. Dorothy Kupcha sold 1,500 copies of her book, *The Big Tomato*, to a large firm relocating employees to the Sacramento area.

It is also easier and less expensive to concoct an advertising campaign when you're just dealing locally. You can put pizzazz in your overall marketing plan with carefully targeted display and classified ads. And if you're doing a high-ticket book, renting a strong local mailing list and creating a direct mail package is something else to consider.

Of course, any author or small publisher is wise to investigate special sales outlets. They frequently provide greater revenue than book stores. Canny people make profitable matches. *The Florida Citrus Cookbook* is sold at fruit stands across the state; while *The California Seafood Book* is peddled at fish markets. Hotel gift shops, military bases, busy real estate offices, restaurants, and shops at tourist attractions are all prime locations for retailing tourist or consumer guides. A children's guide to the city is a natural for children's shops and toy stores. Cookbooks stir up a caldron of interest when placed in gourmet shops or the housewares sections in local department stores. Restaurant guides perch by the cash register at each establishment they review. Beautiful photography books are sold at camera stores. The matches are endless for the innovative merchandiser.

These are just a few ways innovative authors and publishers are cashing in on this new trend in publishing. A well-targeted idea, a quality product, and creative marketing is what it takes to succeed. If you want less reason for hassle—and more opportunity to hustle—regional publishing may be your answer.

Now let's move on to explore the oft ignored world of "op-ed" pages.

10

Newspaper Op-Ed Pages: A Strategic Place to Focus Attention

Those who consider only newspaper book reviews and feature sections when planning how to market their titles are missing an interesting opportunity. Intriguing possibilities also lurk in what are called the "op-ed" (opposite editorial) pages. According to the Newspaper Advertising Bureau, almost 700 daily papers across the country carry them. Op-ed pages consist of guest columns of signed commentaries offering varying viewpoints on topics as diverse as latchkey kids, nuclear arms, and homosexuality.

Going for the Glory

While you can't blatantly tout the name of your book in these columns, you can provoke interest or controversy on the book's *subject*. Additionally, by having the piece go out under your name, you gain added visibility and credibility.

The Trauma of Incest, for instance, offers a powerful potential for a timely piece on child abuse. *The Forest Preserves of New York State: A Conservationist's Handbook* lends itself well to a moving essay on the need for conservation. *You Can Go Home Again,* which deals with the new female mystique, would appeal to editors seeking material on women's issues. And many editors like to print humor on their op-ed pages. Certainly, *101 Uses for an Ex-Husband* has possibilities.

Doing It for Money

But free publicity isn't the sole attraction here. While some smaller papers don't pay anything, the *Los Angeles Times* forks out between $150 and $250. The *Pittsburgh Post-Gazette* rewards contributors with up to $150; and the *Wall Street Journal* admits to three-figure payments. When you consider the majority of editors prefer from 600 to 800 words, that's a reasonable rate of pay.

During the nationwide survey we conducted of some 170 papers with the largest circulations, several editors told us they accept from 5 to 10% of what they receive. That's certainly better odds than freelance submissions to most consumer magazines. And op-ed editors who invite humor and satire provide ideal showcases for poets and humorists who are especially clever with words.

Hows, Whys, and Wherefores

Op-ed editors tell us they prefer a brief cover letter stating your subject, name, and address. Because they work on tight deadlines, they may need to check on an editing change after typical working hours, so include both a day and night phone number. It's also important to include your social security number.

While some papers welcome insights on national and international issues, many prefer a local or regional slant. This need not limit you, however. Out-of-area newspapers, magazines, and electronic news sources can help you find an area news peg. Use it to introduce your concept, then personalize it for that particular op-ed page. So long as you don't infringe on "exclusive" requirements, you can spin out column after column all across the country—garnering repeated exposure, and generating a flurry of checks from all across the country. If this idea appeals to you, get a copy of our *National Survey of Newspaper Op-Ed Pages*.

Now if you *really* want to influence people, the next chapter will be like manna from heaven. It tells you how to go on tour all across the country—yet stay in the comfort of your own home. Sound impossible? Read on.

11

At-Home Radio Interviews: The Primo Publicity Tool

You can talk to literally millions of people over a short time—without ever leaving your home or office. It's really quite simple. You do this by going on the air via your telephone. Yes, radio stations across the land will interview you long distance. And if you do it right, you can sell thousands of books this way.

Another advantage to this way of promoting is you don't have to get in front of the camera or a live mike in a radio station if that makes you uncomfortable. It's kind of like chatting over the phone with a friend. So if you're a shy author who can really identify with why the *Book of Lists* ranks fear of public speaking ahead of death, flying, and loneliness—here's your answer!

Statistics have shown results from radio promotion are often even more impressive than those from TV. First, you have more time to expand upon your subject. On TV, the guest spots usually last less than five minutes. Whereas with radio, many talk shows give you an hour or more. Besides discussing your particular book, you also interact with the audience,

answering questions posed by listeners, and getting
into an extended conversation about the topic.

Not only authors, but small publishers find putting
authors on the air, without either party having to
worry about travel expenses, is an extremely viable
way to sell books. With lower long distance charges,
radio talk shows are now able to team up with a
variety of experts in subject areas from aardvarks to
zoology. Chances are you can be one of these experts.

Prospecting for Appropriate Shows

There are radio stations all across the country that
would welcome you telling your tale. You could do
this virtually all day for months and still not have
reached all of them. However, this isn't what we
suggest. It doesn't make sense to repeatedly spend
hours of your time talking to people in tiny places
like Podunk, Idaho. Unless you need experience, it's
too small an audience. We suggest going for the
numbers. And there's a practical way to do this;
that's one of the secrets we want to reveal to you in
this chapter. There are several different directories
that list radio shows. One we like is *National Radio
Publicity Outlets*. (And we recently heard of a new
one called *Newsclip's Radio Interview Guide*. It is
said to be the first national directory devoted strictly
to telephone interview programs—more than 2,000
of them!) We want to show you how to find the big
time *yourself* instead of paying as much as $1,300 for
someone else to do it for you. Most of the newsletters currently hawking authors to radio shows generate dismal book sales. One publisher did an informal

survey of radio producers to learn about their use of these various services. Her findings showed most producers ignore them.

Those who pin their hopes on these newsletters should realize they are one of dozens being advertised to the radio producers. And again the big names win. Another drawback is that some of these newsletter publishers "work both sides of the street." Not only do they charge authors for listings, they also charge a subscription fee from the radio station. Naturally, the paid subscription ones don't have the circulation base of a newsletter sent free to the stations.

When creating your own mailing, you ideally want to find syndicated or network shows. Some of these go to as many as 1,000 different radio stations around the country! That really makes your time count. Sure the competition is tough. But after you get some experience doing the little Podunk shows, it's time to graduate to the big time. New York and Los Angeles are where most syndicated and network shows originate. In *National Radio Publicity Outlets*, these major shows are listed at the beginning of those two cities. Once you're on the right trail geographically, look at the profile of the shows. Check whether or not the producers schedule telephone interviews. Then create a list of those who do.

There's nothing wrong with doing some smaller stations in out-of-the-way places for practice, to really get your act together and refine it. These are easy enough to find in that directory, or several others as well. Start small and craft a thing of beauty—an interview that is really powerful. Then graduate to the larger shows. Send them an "Avail-

able for Interview" sheet. (See the adjacent visual.)
Prepare a page that tells about you and your subject: three or four succinct points about you as the
expert on the topic, plus four or five points about
the book's subject. Tuck in promotional literature
about the book and offer to send a complimentary
copy.

Remember you are addressing a subject, rather
than talking about a book. You are filling a need—
responding to a problem listeners have. It may be
how to entertain themselves, how to be sexier, how
to be skinnier, how to be healthier, how to be
wealthier. You're not promoting a book; you're
promoting a solution to people's problems. Always
keep that uppermost in your mind. Remember it
when you're creating your "Available for Interview"
sheet, when sending a letter of introduction to the
producer, and when appearing on the show.

"Be Prepared": Motto of the Successful

One of the biggest secrets is to be fully ready.
Mark Twain once said it takes three weeks to prepare a good ad-lib speech. Perhaps the easiest way
to prepare is to do role-playing with yourself and
another individual, or to use a cassette recorder to
tape what you have to say. The point is you need
to get used to talking about your subject in short,
colorful phrases. The idea is to train yourself to
present your message in an abbreviated, punchy way.
Combine clarity with confidence.

Have in mind two or three major points you want
to make. What is the core message of your book?
You need to refine this, hone it, sharpen it until

Contact: Marilyn Ross
(719) 395-8659

COMMUNICATION CREATIVITY

AVAILABLE FOR INTERVIEW

ELIZABETH & DR. ELTON BAKER
authors of

BANDWAGON TO HEALTH: The All-natural Way to Eat, Think and Exercise

ABOUT THE BOOK:

- With six of the ten leading causes of death linked to our diet, Americans have become increasingly concerned about what they eat. Bandwagon to Health shows how to trade conventional habits of food fadism for a wholesome, all-natural way of eating. The authors offer a proven escape from illness, allergy, food pollution, cooking drudgery and skyrocketing food costs.

- It provides a Transitional Diet Program in seven easy phases. This unique book also contains exercises and chapters on kinesiology testing to pinpoint allergies, fasting, how to make your kitchen your garden, plus much, much more.

- This guide deals with The Complete Person. It shows how to nurture body, mind and spirit with an emphasis on the well-functioning body as the essential foundation for a healthy life.

- Bandwagon to Health reveals a potential for total health through an exciting new world of planned menus, savory recipes and down-to-earth information.

ABOUT THE AUTHORS:

- The Bakers are no stranger to the media. They have delighted program personnel and audiences alike on radio, TV and in the press. This dynamic couple were also featured speakers the last two years at the annual convention of the National Health Federation and are scheduled to do a world speaking tour this fall.

- Elizabeth Baker has devoted the last thirteen years to researching and experimenting with nutrition. Diagnosed in 1977 as having terminal cancer of the colon, today -- after making raw food eating a way of life -- her condition has been totally arrested.

- A graduate of Northwestern University, Elizabeth holds a masters degree from Oklahoma State. She previously wrote two novels and co-authored the best-selling UNcook Book. This multi-talented lady has been a nutrition lecturer, teacher and principal.

- Dr. Elton Baker has served as a research scientist at the University of California at Berkeley and as a professor of chemistry at the National University of Bogota, Columbia. Following his stay in that country -- including a stint as advisor to it's National Institute of Nutrition -- he returned to Washington State to chair the Department of Physical Science at Olympia College.

- Currently a Fellow in the International College of Applied Nutrition, and a member of the International Academy of Nutritional Consultants and Northwest Academy of Preventive Medicine, Dr. Baker's life is dedicated to the principles of good health. He has written a newspaper column, "Nutritional News" and co-authored The UNcook Book.

- The Bakers combine scientific expertise with practical know-how. They are provocative spokespersons for the cause of better nutrition and well-being.

P.O. Box 909, 425 Cedar Street, Buena Vista, CO 81211-0909 ● (719) 395-8659 you've got twenty or twenty-five words at the most. It's a good idea to write out this "mission statement." Choose forceful words. Use the active voice. Then literally memorize it—not so it becomes a rote announcement, but rather a lively and precise declaration.

Practice aloud. We see things differently with our eyes than we hear them with our ears. As you're role-playing, also get in the habit of presenting your main point right at the very beginning. Don't wander into an interview. Dive in! Say something stimulating. The same rules that apply to good writing apply to good interviewing. You must capture the imagination and the interest of the audience at the onset.

It is a good idea to get in the habit of making a short statement or giving a brief answer, then elaborating on it. That way if you are put in a position where time is limited, you've already said the most important thing. When you're on a more leisurely show you can then expound by sharing an anecdote, telling a story, giving a case history, or in some way embellishing your initial statement.

Don't try to become too perfect though. You don't want to sound like a polished speaker or a suave politician. Be human. Strive to come across as someone who's deeply involved in the subject. Excited. Enthusiastic. Forthright. It's much more important on a longer radio show to be captivatingly conversational than perfectly polished.

If your subject lends itself, try to think of something that would be easy for the average listener to understand and relate to. For instance, a computer company explained, "Today we can put all the intelligence of a room-sized computer from the 1950s into a silicon chip the size of a corn flake." Not everyone relates to silicon chips, but everybody understands corn flakes. Look at your own subject. See what you can find that makes it easy for the average person to grasp.

Don't be afraid to let people get to know the real you. If you love sports, why not use an analogy about football or baseball? Or if you're a music buff, perhaps you want to use a comparison to an orchestra or a jazz band. Allow listeners to learn a little bit about you as a person. After all, authors are perceived as glamorous, exciting people. Don't you want to reinforce that image?

Setting the Stage

Now that we've talked about the preparation you're going to do for your actual verbal presentation, let's discuss another kind of preparation. There are two items you should create before you ever go on the radio. First is a set of 3 x 5 inch cards, three for each interview. They should contain the name of the book, the author, the publisher, the price, and ordering information. You're going to send these to prime people before you go on the air so they have them in their hot little hands when your interview occurs. These cards go to the following: (1) to the producer of the show, (2) to the host or hostess who will be interviewing you, and (3) to the station switchboard operator or the phone receptionist. For the switchboard operator, also put a little flag on the card noting when you're going to be interviewed. Also write a notation that this is for her convenience so if calls come in about the book, the information is readily at hand. By doing this you've helped these people to help you. Make it easy for them to direct people to you for orders.

The other item we're going to create is some sort of a giveaway, a "freebie" you can announce and make available while you're being interviewed. It doesn't have to be elaborate, just a one-pager will do. Americans love trivia. Why not create a trivia quiz from information in your book? Or perhaps there's some sort of list that would be helpful to people. Maybe it's a four-page booklet that gives an overview of the subject. Your giveaway should be something of value or a fun, intriguing gift for your listeners. Notice the adjacent "Baker's Dozen Natural Health Quiz," which we developed for one of our authors.

Be sure to include full book ordering information on your giveaway. Of course, you'll include a consumer brochure too—a *benefit-oriented* customer order form like the one we discussed in an earlier chapter.

You've just discovered the big secret for getting orders from radio interviews! (We'll tell you how to introduce your "freebie" shortly.) Oh sure, some people will go to bookstores. If you or your publisher are aggressive about getting books placed in the area, that's wonderful. But very often it isn't practical. If you live in Miami, for instance, how do you personally see that books are stocked in every bookstore in the Northwest if that's where the show is airing. By offering a giveaway, you encourage people to get in touch with you directly. You provide a way for listeners to get your book without having to go to bookstores or being frustrated because they can't find it.

BAKER'S DOZEN NATURAL HEALTH QUIZ

1) Name the miracle energy booster. (page 73)

2) What is one of the key nutrients in the prevention and recovery from cancer? (page 48)

3) What do hyperactive children need to give up to become calm? (page 102)

4) Name the most exciting thing happening today in the treatment of epilepsy. (page 73)

5) Why is homogenized milk harmful? (page 114)

6) What four things can you take to curb nausea and hair loss from radiation treatments? (page 142)

7) Name the vitamin that helps scars and acne heal quickly. (page 143)

8) What is a fool-proof way to determine the proper dosage of vitamins and minerals? (page 227)

9) What can you give your baby to get it over colic? (page 58)

10) What fruit is especially good for a cleansing fast to rid the body of impurities? (page 71)

11) The increase in heart attacks has consistently gone up as the ingestion of what vitamin has gone down? (page 95)

12) What new non-surgical treatment is being used for hemorrhoids? (page 97)

13) How can you discover more about these things -- and much, much more?

ANSWERS:

1) spirulina plankton
2) vitamin C
3) sugar and processed foods
4) nutrition -- it is a deficiency disease
5) because it contains xanthine oxidase, which is broken down when homogenized
6) vitamins C, E, A and yeast
7) vitamin E
8) use Kinesiology Testing
9) potassium chloride
10) watermelon
11) vitamine E
12) negative galvanic current
13) by getting a copy of <u>The UNmedical Book: How to Conquer Disease, Lose Weight, Avoid Suffering & Save Money</u> by Elizabeth and Dr. Elton Baker. (Available for $8.95, plus $2 shipping, from Communication Creativity, Box 213R, Saguache, CO 81149.)

Now you're ready to go on the air.

The Curtain Rises

It's extremely important to be lively and animated. Put yourself in the audience's position. If a guest starts in a monotone, disinterested voice, you fail to become excited as well. Be dynamic in that first minute or two when you're welcomed by the host or hostess. Be passionate about your message! Begin with something important. Remember, you are the authority on your book's subject—that's why you're being interviewed. It's essential you show that expertise in your explanations.

One of the biggest flaws that occurs in most interviews is the author typically talks about "my book." It's my book this and my book that. Unfortunately this doesn't help listeners interested in buying that specific book. Name your book! You don't have to reiterate the title every other sentence, but several times throughout your interview you will have opportunities to gracefully introduce the title of your book. You can do this by saying, "In chapter fourteen of the *Complete Guide to Self-Publishing* I cover...." or you might say "What people tell us they like most about the *Complete Guide to Self-Publishing* is...." These are just two examples. There are all kinds of ways to weave in the title of your book. Think about it and have some ready.

Get the name of the person who will be interviewing you ahead of time; use his or her name as you talk. It gives the interview a more personal touch. Remember, however, that you're not talking to only that individual. You're addressing the entire audience. And you should frame your comments for all listeners, not just the host.

Don't overlook the opportunity for capitalizing on controversy. If you can link your subject to a timely, current issue—or use it as a springboard to discuss something controversial in the news—by all means do so. Controversy presents an opportunity for wonderful interaction with your listeners. A talk show really hums when you get a lot of audience involvement. Of course, when you're dealing with controversy, there will be times when you're asked difficult questions. Keep your cool. Some interviewers will deliberately try to trip you. As long as you know your subject well and stay calm, you're not likely to get into trouble.

Let us share with you a good tactic when you're asked a question you don't quite know how to deal with. Use a stalling phrase. One technique is to simply repeat the question. Another good ploy is to say to the host or hostess, "You know, John, that's a very good question." As you're saying this, your mind has a chance to regroup and decide on an appropriate reply.

What do you do when the host or hostess starts rambling and gets totally off the subject, focusing the show in a direction of no value to you? Take a lesson from Jacqueline Susann. She was a master at handling the media. If an interviewer tried to get her onto a topic she didn't like, she'd say something like, "You know, that's a fascinating subject. It reminds me of a chapter in my novel...." And she'd be right back on track with her book. We can use that same strategy to help the host or hostess stay on the subject we're there to discuss.

Most women need to be conscious of their voice level. Ladies tend to talk in too high a pitch. Practice lowering your voice if you're a female. Variety is important for everyone. Project a tone that is both low and occasionally high. Consider pacing—say some things rapidly; state important points slowly and emphatically.

It's also useful when you're actually on the air to think about where this show is being aired. For instance, if you're talking to a Midwest audience, they're typically going to be turned off by casual attitudes towards sex and marriage. If you're addressing people in southern California, they have a much more relaxed and open attitude toward most subjects. If it's a nationally syndicated or network show airing many places around the country, play it safe.

We mentioned before about creating a giveaway. Now's the time to bring it into play. Towards the end of the interview, it's appropriate for you to comment, "By the way, John, I've created something I think many of your listeners would like to have." State you have a free gift you'd like to make available (naming whatever it is). Explain that to get a copy all they have to do is send a self-addressed, stamped envelope. Then give your address. Make the address as simple and quick as possible. Rather than saying "P. O. Box 3789," just say, "Box 3789". Instead of giving a long, complicated name for the publisher, say "Free Gift" or something of the sort. Don't take up a lot of time on the address. Ideally you want to be able to repeat it, so make it as easy as possible.

If conducting a telephone interview is nerve-racking for you, there are things you can do to make yourself more comfortable. One is to have handy some slightly warm water laced with a little lemon juice in it. This is a trick professional speakers use; it helps lubricate your throat. Something else to do if you're very tense is to use a bit of petroleum jelly to moisten the underside of your lips. When doing a phone interview, have something available to drink. Talking for an hour can be a strain for anyone. Before beginning, take a couple of big deep breaths and exhale slowly to relax.

After the Curtain Falls

An important follow-up to your interview, something often neglected, is a thank you. Send a brief note to both the producer and the host. Surprisingly, this is seldom done. It's not only polite, but wise. If you have done well on a radio show, it's quite possible you'll be invited back in a few months. This has been the experience of many of our clients. And if you've used this way of staying in touch with people, they're going to be thinking more favorably toward you. So remember to follow up media engagements with a note of appreciation.

Another wise thing is to have the interview taped. If you don't tape it on your end, you can always send a cassette to the radio station ahead of time and ask them to tape the interview. Listen carefully to that interview. Critique it. What did you do well? Where were you particularly outstanding? And what do you need to improve upon? You can learn much from listening to your interviews. You'll be better once you've evaluated strengths and weaknesses—and taken steps to improve them.

Yes, remote radio interviews offer an unprecedented, free way to sell books. We have now given you the tools to take advantage of this opportunity. Use them wisely, to increase your visibility and profitability.

Now let's move on to some penetrating questions and answers.

12

More Publicizing Techniques for Authors and Publishers

Pinning Down Publicity: An Interview with Marilyn Ross

Because it answers so many of the questions that haunt authors and self-publishers, we have been asked to include this interview, which first appeared in the COSMEP Newsletter. COSMEP is the international association of independent presses. The interviewer is John B. McHugh, author of the McHugh Publishing Reports, a series of practical guides for the publishing manager and self-publisher.

JM: Is advertising the same as publicity?

MR: Definitely not. You pay for advertising; publicity is free. And there's a lot of it out there for the shrewd publisher or author who knows how to tap into it.

JM: Which is more effective for the book publisher, advertising or publicity?

MR: That depends on the book. One selling for $20 or more, for instance, may do better with display advertising or a direct-marketing campaign. You have enough profit built in on a high-ticket book to pay for costly advertising techniques. But for the average book, publicity is dynamite. It's an impartial, third-party endorsement. The consumer knows it is not you paying for advertising, but rather someone else saying your book is good. That packs a real wallop.

JM: How can the self-publisher or small trade publisher be more effective in publicizing books than the large rich New York City trade publisher? After all, the New York City publisher has more money, more people, more expertise and more contacts.

MR: First, the small publisher really cares. He or she has one or a few books to work on, not hundreds. Each is special and important.

Second, the wise independent publisher has chosen the subject carefully, only doing a book where there is an easily identified; targeted market. That target market can be reached effectively and inexpensively.

Third, the smaller publisher can maintain control over everyday operations, making sure promotional strategies are maintained. Big publishers are too busy to handle such details. They forget that reviewers are often overworked, rushed people. We teach our seminar attendees and clients to make the reviewer's job as easy as possible—include a punchy news release and a mock-up review that you've written. I can't tell you how many times the reviews

EXPANDED BEST-SELLER OFFERS SUCCESSFUL BOOK PUBLISHING, MARKETING TIPS

The Complete Guide to Self-Publishing: Everything You Need to Know to Write, Publish, Promote, and Sell Your Own Book by Tom and Marilyn Ross. $16.95, 420-page trade paperback. Writer's Digest Books, distributed by Communication Creativity, Box 909, Buena Vista, CO 81211. Appendix, bibliography, glossary, index. ISBN 0-89879-354-8, LCCN 85-8224.

The subtitle says it all: "Everything You Need to Know to Write, Publish, Promote, and Sell Your Own Book." And it delivers on that promise. The newly revised and expanded paperback edition of *The Complete Guide to Self-Publishing* is a whopping 420 pages of detailed, step-by-step instructions covering the A to Z of successfully launching a book. Nationally known for their book consulting service and publishing seminars, authors Tom and Marilyn Ross draw upon their own experience to create a reference work rich in information, proven advice, and innovative marketing ideas.

A look at bookstore shelves shows many are putting pen to paper these days. Professionals, entrepreneurs, associations and countless others are using this method to reach larger audiences with their particular message. But, as noted industry authority John P. Dessauer states in his foreword to the Rosses' best-seller: "The U.S. Constitution guarantees freedom to publish, but does not provide everyone with the talents, skills and resources necessary to publish successfully." To accomplish this, my advice is to pick up a copy of *The Complete Guide to Self-Publishing*.

Divided into 120 fact-filled sections, this comprehensive how-to handbook begins with the writing process. The Rosses give sound advice for choosing a marketable subject, researching it, and producing tight, snappy copy. Next they tell how to set up a publishing venture and cover operating procedures. The completely updated overview of personal computers gives the latest word on the most effective desktop publishing systems, databases, laser printers, and word processing programs.

The real meat of the book lies in the insider's view of the publishing and marketing process. The authors know exactly what needs to be done and when to do it. They tell how to secure important catalog numbers and get advance listings. The ins and outs of book design, production, and manufacturing are explained, along with tips for ensuring professional results whether authors do most of the work themselves or contract it out.

General advertising pointers advise how to write sales materials with punch, get free "PI" ads, and promote to target audiences. Other innovative techniques are discussed, such as mail-order ads and direct marketing. Publicity and promotion can make a book; readers are shown how to garner free exposure from reviewers, associations, and media people.

Getting a book into the standard channels of distribution—bookstores, wholesalers, libraries, and schools—is discussed. Since many books soar to success through less conventional channels, these are explored in depth. The pros and cons of working with trade publishers, agents, and subsidy (vanity) publishers round out the book. A useful publishing countdown timetable summarizes the process. Comprehensive appendices provide reference information.

Throughout, the Rosses stimulate creative marketing ideas. They show how anyone interested in producing and selling a book can go about it successfully. Additionally, trade-published authors unhappy with the lack of attention their book is receiving will learn what to do about it. Even trade publishers stand to gain new promotional ideas. *The Complete Guide to Self-Publishing* always was a must resource. Now it's even better.

published about books we represent are re-works of what *we* provided.

JM: If a person is an author and not a self-publisher, why should that person take the responsibility for publicizing his/her book? After all, isn't that the responsibility of the publisher? Don't publishers publicize all of their books?

MR: Authors should only get involved with publicity if they want to make more money than just the initial advance. While in theory it is the publisher's job to publicize a book, real life simply doesn't work that way unless you're Jean Auel or Sidney Sheldon. Most books are considered "mid-list"—that means the publishing house has no great expectations for them. Oh, the marketing department may spend a few days and a few dollars marketing them. Then it's wait and see. If the book is lucky enough to take off, they'll fan the fire. Otherwise, forget it. The author's chances of ever getting more than the initial advance are mighty slim. Yet authors can have a dramatic impact on the success of their book—if they know what to do and are willing to invest a little time and energy.

JM: In starting a publicity campaign for a book, when and where should one begin?

MR: Before the book is ever written. I know that sounds ridiculous to a lot of our readers, but shrewd independent publishers do a lot of planning before they ever sit down to pound out the manuscript. A book—even though it is your precious baby—is a product. And, as such, it needs to be "positioned."

That means you must make it uniquely fill a need no other book currently does. A book we are currently writing is about advertising and publicity. Yet a look in *Subject Guide to Books in Print* could discourage that idea in a hurry. There are pages and pages of such titles listed. None of them, however, addresses the special needs of *service* businesses. That is what our book is about: *Big Marketing Ideas for Small Service Businesses*. We found a niche to fill; we've positioned our product. You should, too.

Another thing you can do in the early stages to help publicity is to "seed" your book with certain editorial material. Maybe you will mention a person, place, or organization that will later help promote your book. Something else my husband, Tom, and I recommend is to solicit a prominent person to write a Foreword. Their name recognition will help carry the book if properly publicized.

JM: What's the first step for a new self-publisher?

MR: Explore all your options. Really do some creative brainstorming. Capture every idea on paper or cassette no matter how far-out it seems. Plan on cuddling up with the reference volumes in a good library for a couple of days. Then organize your publicity ideas into categories and prioritize them, giving those likely to return the greatest exposure the largest part of your time.

And forget what mother always told you about not "blowing your own horn." It is imperative that you—or someone you hire—talk about the merits of your book. You'll need to develop promotional materials with pizzazz, so polish up your writing skills, too. Remember to stress the benefits your book will provide the potential reader.

JM: Assuming that everyone's time (and capital) are limited, what would you say are the three most important publicity techniques?

MR: 1) Key reviews—because so many in the bookselling and library trade rely on them to make buying decisions. Also, reviews in targeted, specialized publications can generate a flood of orders. For instance, we recently published a small directory called *The National Survey of Newspaper "Op-Ed" Pages*. It is especially useful for public relations professionals, so I did a press release campaign to newsletter editors in PR and related fields. As a direct result of that news release, we've sold hundreds of copies of the survey, all without spending one cent on advertising.
2) Word-of-mouth—there isn't one specific thing you can do to create this. It comes, or doesn't, as a result of people hearing of your book and getting excited about it. It is typically the result of a cumulative PR effort, so don't overlook any angle to get your book mentioned—anywhere. You never know who might be reading, watching, or listening.
3) Personal contacts—smart business people in all industries cultivate a network of like-minded folks who can help them, and whom they assist. Look over your Christmas card list, go through your Rolodex or business card file, talk to friends and colleagues. Ask for their help in promoting your book. They may know key people such as the producer of a TV show, a staff writer at a magazine, or

an executive at a corporation who might be interested in bulk quantities of your book.

JM: Do you have an example or two of unique, inexpensive publicity that effectively sold books?

MR: I'm a great believer in syndicated columnists. There are people who write nationally distributed columns on virtually every conceivable topic. Your job is to ferret them out and let them know about your exciting new book. We did this for one client with especially rewarding results. A syndicated columnist wrote a glowing dissertation about *I Want to Change but I Don't Know How*, and we filled almost 500 orders as a result.

JM: How did you learn to publicize books? Did you work in the publicity department of a book publisher? Do you have an advertising background?

MR: I've always found PR a challenging and exciting creative process and I guess we do best at what we enjoy. I worked as the Director of Marketing for a large west coast vocational school for five years. That's where I got lots of hands-on experience writing promotional copy, developing PR and ad concepts, and strategizing. I've also had my own advertising and PR agency. In 1977, writing and selling freelance articles lost its glow and I decided to publish my own book. From that emerged more books, Tom's and my titles on self-publishing, our consulting service, and our nationwide seminars on how to successfully publish and promote books.

JM: Any other comments, advice or observations for publicizing books?

MR: Yes. I'd like to leave our readers with a couple of important ideas: be persistent! Follow-up is vital for success. Don't just do something once and wait for the world to come knocking.

And be sure to milk your publicity for all it's worth. When you get a good review or something exciting breaks, make copies of it and send it to all your distributors, other potential reviewers, anyone who you're trying to influence.

Spotlight on the Author/Publisher/Consultant

The following interview with Marilyn and Tom Ross first appeared in The Griffin *Signature* newsletter. Although the discussion concerns self-publishers, it contains much information of value to all authors.

GS: What consistent mistakes, no matter how much they are counselled otherwise, do self-publishers tend to make over and over?

MARILYN: One of the biggest mistakes is poor choice of subject. The average person does not really think about the marketability of his subject before he gets started. He fails to find out if there is a need for this type of book; if he can reach the target audience. You are much better off with a closely-defined subject.

For instance, a book on dog training can be useful because you can readily find your market; you can reach the niche of people who are interested in that particular subject. You can do it as a possible premium for a dog food manufacturer. You can sell it to kennels or to breeders, at dog shows, pet shops and things like that. If you're looking to get into a financially viable situation, that kind of book—though it may not sound as glamorous as others—is much better for the smaller publisher than a general interest book. It is a lot easier to focus on your subject and to narrow it down to a readily-identifiable target market.

Another important thing, obviously, is the pricing of a book. If you don't know the formulas and adhere to them, it can absolutely kill you. We have people come to us who say, "My costs are five dollars per book, so I'm going to sell it for ten dollars," which is ludicrous! You have to charge a minimum of five times the cost of the book, and much more comfortably eight times, especially for your initial run. And if the figures are not there, then you have to sit down with someone and find out if there are ways to get a better price. Are there ways to change the format of the book, or is it a viable project? But pricing is crucial to success. Some small publishers are simply writers or authors who decided to become business people. And writers are wonderfully creative souls, but the majority of them don't have sound business understanding. They must educate themselves if they are going into publishing because it is a business.

GS: With all of the renewed interest in books and in book publishing, is it harder or easier to get your book promoted these days?

TOM: There is a combination of things that make it much harder to get media exposure today than, say, ten years ago. First, there are a lot more publishers; this industry has grown tremendously over the past few years. Another thing is, it seems virtually every movie star, television star, sports figure, CEO, or industry leader is writing a book of some sort. So the competition is tremendous.

What we often help people do is to get on radio. Radio stations are still amenable to the author, and very often from your office you can give extremely productive radio interviews. So we will put together a plan doing that, among other things. You just have to be more creative, more tenacious, have more follow-through. I feel that is one of the mistakes people make in this business—in fact in any business. They don't follow through with something they believe in, they just don't stick with it.

MARILYN: For example, one of the clients who we have been distributing for since 1980, has a nutrition book. When we approached him, the main specialty wholesaler for that kind of book said, "No, absolutely not. I handle too many of those books already. I don't want any more." Well, I just pestered this poor guy to death in as nice a way as I could. Every time we got a review, I sent him a copy. Every time we got a letter from a reader who loved it, I sent him a copy.

Finally, he ordered a case of books—just to get me off his back, I'm sure. But interestingly enough, it's directly through his sales that the book is in its fifth printing. Now he orders cases and cases of books every month and is thrilled to death because it's one of his best sellers. But if I hadn't stayed on it because I felt it was so right, nothing would have happened. Of course, you don't want to go after everyone like that, but if you feel something is a perfect match, don't give up. *Tactfully* stay in front of that wholesaler, reviewer, or bookstore in every way you can.

TOM: It is so important to put together a marketing plan before you spend time writing a whole book. Find out how you're going to slant it, if there is a need for it, and know what you're going to do with it. Very often you can plant things in the writing process that gives it additional exposure, from a marketing standpoint, further downstream.

MARILYN: You need to find out where you're going before you get there. You wouldn't jump on a plane to take a trip without having some idea where you were going. So very often with a book people will just sit down and take off on their trip without having any specific destination in mind. This can be disastrous. So we really try to stress with people to give thorough consideration to marketing before they get very far in their project.

TOM: Of course, this presupposes you want to be successful. Not everyone publishes for the same reason. Some people publish from an egotistical standpoint, some for a specific cause, but most of us publish to make money. It may sound a little money-hungry, but most of us publish, not only for the sheer joy of it, but also for the financial reward from it. If that is your motivation, then you have to do your homework. No one else would go out and create a product without doing a market research study, and yet authors and small publishers do that all the time. A book is a product. You have to address it from that aspect and make sure there is a market for that product.

Of course sometimes, if you can't find a market—and maybe this is a harsh thing for someone who is an advocate of self-publishing to say—but sometimes that's a blessing in disguise. Maybe you had just better not be publishing that book.

GS: People seem so infatuated with (or leery of) desktop publishing they fail to realize some of the other benefits that computers bring to the business of publishing. In what other areas do you find them most helpful?

MARILYN: Computers are wonderful from a writing and editing standpoint. I have more than doubled my productivity since I became computerized. They are also a tremendous boon to marketing because you can integrate your letters with mailing lists and print labels. Then, of course, there are the business programs for accounting, inventory control, databases and so on. I totally believe every writer or publisher should have a personal computer. I do not, however, advocate that they should necessarily run right out and arbitrarily get desktop publishing. (In the new revised and expanded paperback edition of our *Complete Guide to Self-Publishing*, we explore this subject in detail and make buying recommendations.)

TOM: We feel that desktop publishing is going to be immensely viable in a couple more years. In many cases it is today, but the technology is improving so rapidly that in another few years everything is going to cost so much less, it really is going to be practical.

But on the other side a lot of people get into desktop publishing without realizing what it involves. You practically have to learn to be a typesetter. You have to learn to spec type, how to graphically design, and it just isn't as simple as keyboarding in a manuscript. The poor guy who is basically just a writer, and isn't talented visually, is going to have a terrible time relating to that while trying to get the system to work properly. There's a learning curve to everything we do. Even a person who *isn't* totally naive to the techniques of graphic design and the use of computers applications really has his work cut out for him. Especially if he plans to use desktop technology to compete on a professional level with other publishers.

GS: In your book, *How to Make Big Profits Publishing City and Regional Books*, you recommend library sales as desirable, while many self-publishers tend to avoid them like the plague. How come?

MARILYN: I think it's such a mistake to avoid libraries. So many times people will see your book in the library and decide they want their own personal copy. I can't tell you how many people have written us about our *Complete Guide to Self-Publishing* to say they've worn out the library copy and want their own. I have never found that library sales detract. Everything you can do to get people to know about your book, you're better off. I find if people are serious about that subject, very often they will get the book themselves, or they'll talk about it with others. If it isn't in the library, everyone loses. Naturally, it depends on the type of book. This would not be true of a novel. How-to or reference books fall into this category much better.

GS: Your books and seminars are high on the recommendations list for fledgling self-publishers, but what about the old-timers? As a publishing consultant, what are the types of problems that you see them facing the most, and how do you help them?

MARILYN: I think it's too easy for most of us to get stale after we have been doing it for a while. We lose that spark of enthusiasm, and we get too comfortable in our little ruts. We don't necessarily look at all of the creative ways of doing things. We don't stay as fresh as we could in marketing our books.

TOM: My advice to long-time publishers is to try to stay in touch with what is going on around you—and not just in your own particular little niche. See what the other guy is doing out there and try to relate it to your own endeavors. We do a lot of experimenting ourselves to see what works and what doesn't.

MARILYN: We belong to several publishing groups including COSMEP, Publishers Marketing Association, the National Association of Independent Publishers, Rocky Mountain Book Publishers Association, and many others. We very much believe in supporting these groups because we keep abreast by reading their newsletters and benefit from the contacts we make at conventions, book shows, and seminars.

We also subscribe to virtually everything that has to do with the industry. And we network with other professionals to find out what they're doing and how it has worked for them. Another thing is to keep good records of your promotional strategies. Follow through on the ones that are most effective and junk the rest.

GS: Are there any new areas of interest for self-publishers?

MARILYN: Audiotape represents an alternative media market opening up for some self-publishers. I say some because certain markets do not lend themselves to the audio medium while others do. For certain books it's an excellent thing. We're seeing more and more of this because we have become such a commuter society where people can listen to tapes as they drive to work. It's an easy way to learn. I'm not sure whether it's viable or not from an entertainment standpoint, but it certainly is from a learning or how-to aspect.

TOM: We've just completed our cassette tape program *Book Promotion and Marketing*. The official publication date is just this month, and we are very excited about it because it is the newest thing on the subject. We spend six hours looking at everything from direct mail campaigns to garnering reviews. The tape program also covers much other specific information. It comes with a workbook that has current names and addresses.

The Ross Idea Generator:
44 Winning Strategies

- Request complimentary review copies from your publisher.

- Try to find an angle that will make your book controversial.

- Do radio phone interviews originating from your home/office.

- Go after TV (not everyone can crack Oprah or Donahue).

- Pursue newspaper features about your subject/book.

- Write op-ed pieces addressing the subject.

- Submit letters to the editor piggybacking on related articles.

- Plant news items with local newspaper/magazine columnists.

- Provide gratis articles to national magazines.

- Solicit reviews/plugs in newsletters.

- Go after mentions by nationally syndicated newspaper columnists.

- Develop association alliances for reviews and bulk sales.

- Request testimonials from leaders in the industry.

- Create a sales flyer and customer order form.

- Prepare a "Here's What People Are Saying" flyer of comments.

- Do mailings to your Christmas/address book lists.

- Pitch your book at your publishers' sales rep conference.

- Make presentations to key wholesalers' sales forces.

- Generate a mailing list of interested professionals.

- Position your book as a premium item.

- Pursue second serial/excerpt rights sales.

- Investigate non-bookstore special sales outlets.

- Create an "event" centered around your book.

- Establish an award that correlates with your book's subject.

- Tie in with a special national or day/week/month.

- Set up drop-ship deals.

- Establish "P.I." (Per Inquiry) advertising arrangements.

- Go after specialty book clubs.

- Regularly communicate with key wholesalers/distributors.

- Print bookmarks and give them to area bookstores.

- Autograph inventory left in area bookstores.

- Speak about your topic and sell books afterward.

- Look for a way to give in-store demonstrations.

- Do co-op mailings with other authors of complementary books.

- Produce buttons to promote your book in/out of the publishing house.

- Provide books to area radio stations to use as giveaways.

- Be alert to news events and hot issues you can piggyback on.

- Get your book included in appropriate bibliographies.

- Seek out catalogs that sell related merchandise and contact them.

- Enter any contests for which you qualify.

- Consider museums, national historic sites, etc., as sales outlets.

- Donate a copy to your main branch library and publicize your action.

- Take out inexpensive classified ads in targeted magazines.

- Follow up, follow up, follow up!

13

Controlling Your Time to Maximize Your Results

There's an adage that goes, "If you want to get a job done, give it to a busy person." Why is it those individuals who already seem overloaded can always manage to squeeze in one more task? The secret is, they've learned to maximize their time. We may envy such highly organized go-getters, but this skill can be mastered by anyone. Time Management is essential if you're going to successfully market your books.

Time is money. It's a valuable commodity. How it's used can spell failure or success. Productive people manage their time, rather than letting it manage them.

Writers are renowned for passing hours sharpening pencils or staring at blank computer screens. The truth is, we have the same problems as everyone else. And the solutions are universal too. Let's explore them.

Getting Focused

To make the best use of your time, you have to decide first what is important. What are your goals? Your highest priority? If you've decided to put together a powerful direct mail package, don't get sidetracked going after secondary review sources. Likewise, if you've determined a nationwide radio campaign makes sense, don't dilute your effectiveness by trying to set up fund-raising deals with area churches. Get the idea? When there is a question of your taking time for a certain activity, ask yourself, will this particular activity (whatever it is) further my goals? Will it be an opportunity or a burden? Will it put my objectives on hold? Do it only if it supports your overall plan. Learn to say no. That will be the end to "Let good old George—or Georgia—do it" and the beginning of getting where *you* want to go.

Reading on the Run

Many of us subscribe to important trade journals and newsletters to keep abreast of developments in our field. But you needn't take a chunk of time out of your prime work day to read them. Instead, tuck these materials in to read when you go to the doctor's office, to scan on a plane, to review while waiting for a meeting to begin, or your kids to get out of school. Experts estimate we spend 15 to 30 minutes a day waiting in some line or other. That can amount to 200 hours a year! Why not keep a folder of reading in your briefcase, purse, or car? Then you can use precious time that would otherwise be wasted.

If there's something you want to learn, an effective method is via audio cassettes. And what better time to listen than when you're commuting? Then even being stuck in traffic loses its sting. Here's what John Kremer of Ad Lib Publications says about our audio program, *Book Promotion and Marketing*: "Put these tapes on while you drive to work, or pack books, or eat lunch. Each time I listen to these tapes I come up with new ways to sell books."

Turning the Phone from Foe to Friend

The phone is a time gobbler that must be controlled. When making calls, avoid Monday morning or Friday afternoon if at all possible. People are either involved in meetings on Mondays or already gone for the weekend Friday, so you'll just have to call again. If you're lucky enough to have a secretary, that's who you may want to place the call, taking over yourself once the other person is on the line. If your job involves a lot of calls where you're left hanging on hold, try keeping a folder on your desk where you stash quickie work, like checks and letters needing your signature. Then the waiting time will be put to productive use.

Most of us are unintentional captives to incoming calls. This doesn't make sense. If you're in the middle of a meeting where several other people will be kept idle while you take the call, a message is usually preferable. If you find personal calls frequently interrupt your writing flow, explain to friends and loved ones this is diluting your effectiveness. Schedule certain times to receive calls—let people know what they are—and stick to them. We all decry the inhumanity of answering machines. But they are the redeemers of privacy, productivity, and efficiency. If all else fails, turn on the answering machine and turn off the telephone.

Another technique is to batch your outgoing calls. It takes less time to make all your research or marketing follow-up calls at one time than it does to strew them through the day like wild mushrooms across a field. A telephone can be a lifeline to the world—or a chain that keeps you tethered to its whim. You hold the key to making it serve *you* rather than you serving it.

Finding Your Pattern

Another way to sabotage yourself is to procrastinate. All of us have personal power patterns, times when we're freshest and most productive. Find yours. If it's in the morning, tackle the more demanding tasks then, when you're at your prime. Get your most inspired writing or brightest marketing ideas late at night? Set aside those hours. By prioritizing this way, the time when you're least effective is saved for more routine work, while your overall productivity increases.

A different kind of pattern to establish is one for routine chores, such as paying bills on the fifteenth and the thirtieth, calling to verify appointments the first of each week, and so on. When you have a set time for these things, they don't buzz at the edge of your mind, disturbing your concentration and stealing your time.

Organize to Maximize

Of course, economies in time aren't relegated to business or home office environments. Sometimes their absence is easier to spot elsewhere.

How often have you gone into a restaurant and watched a waitress bring you water, then return to the kitchen empty-handed—leaving a nearby table cluttered with dirty dishes? Had she made her trip count and taken some dirty dishes along, she'd be less tired by days end. Clerks in retail stores could be more efficient if they would ask a customer at the outset about *all* his or her needs. Then, while walking through the store to point out or pick up items, a regulated pattern could be established.

The same procedures can work for you. Instead of running around in a frenzy on Saturday, why not stop by the post office for stamps on the way to work; drop into the library to do some research or return books on the way home? If you don't have to wait in line, your time can be put to much better use, so take advantage of off hours. Bank early in the morning, grocery shop in the evening. Think ahead, and you'll save time and energy you can expend in making more money from your writing.

The placement of equipment, whether in a fancy office or a corner of your bedroom reserved for writing, can also affect time. Let's use the example of the restaurant again: how often have you waited impatiently for the waitress to bring coffee from a stand located far from the one where she just got your water? Or run to get your change from the cash register at the back? Efficient use of time dictates having coffee, water, and cash register strategically placed to save steps. Likewise, how did you feel as you watched that repairman you were paying by the hour backtrack constantly because needed tools weren't at hand?

Think through your tasks and decide what things you use most frequently, then place them within easy reach. If they are small items, organize them in containers. The more organized you become, the more time you have to concentrate on your goals.

Systems Geared for Success

If you're like most people, you waste a lot of time looking for things you know you have but can't find. Setting up a simple system could wipe this aggravation from your life forever. What do you need to put you in control?

Each of us prefers different methods to keep track of things. Many of the best cooks keep all their pots and pans hanging in plain sight. Other cooks, just as good, store them in cupboards. Either approach is valid. One person's system is another's chaos.

The point is to establish some sort of tracking process. It may be manila folders, colored binders, three by five file cards with notations, dates and activities penned on a calendar, lucite see-through box files, perhaps a special drawer or shelf. Develop some system to control the whirl of paperwork surrounding every job and every life. Then be sure to *use* that system.

By applying these few tips, you should be able to minimize your frustrations and maximize your time, thus better controlling your destiny. What's more, you'll *feel* efficient. (Which is sometimes half the battle.) A word of caution, though: the key to efficiency is in not always adhering strictly to the program. Don't waste time pursuing perfectionism. A little flexibility can sometimes result in a big spurt of productivity. As Emerson said, "This time, like all times, is a very good one, if we but know what to do with it."

About the Authors

For over a decade Tom and Marilyn Ross have helped hundreds of authors, entrepreneurs, associations, and professionals successfully publish and promote their books. They are pictured here with some of the projects they have worked on through their consulting firm, About Books, Inc. The Rosses are perhaps best known for their *Complete Guide to Self-Publishing*. This bestselling title was recently released by Writers Digest Books in a revised, expanded paperback edition.

These busy professionals continue to be in demand as speakers. They've been on the faculty of

Folio's New York Face to Face conference, spoken at colleges and universities, and are often called upon by writing and publishing groups to be keynote speakers or to present seminars.

Marilyn Ross is the award-winning author of nine nonfiction books. She has also been a corporate director of marketing and owned and operated her own advertising/PR agency. Marilyn is a member of the National Speakers Association, the American Society of Journalists and Authors, and serves as chairperson of COSMEP. She is listed in many who's who directories, including *Who's Who of American Women*.

Tom Ross has masterminded promotional campaigns which created extensive print, radio, and TV coverage—plus opened doors for national book distribution. As a consultant, Tom specializes in helping clients with project analysis, production, computerization, and developing nationwide book marketing campaigns. He is a member of the American Management Association and is listed in *Who's Who in the West*.

Marilyn and Tom have a proven track record of producing attractive books and result-getting promotion and publicity. They can be reached by contacting About Books, Inc., at Box 1500-MYB, Buena Vista, CO 81211 or by calling (719) 395-2459.

Index

Q

R

S

U

W

Y

T

Did You Borrow This Book? Want a Copy of Your Own?

Need a Great Gift for a Friend or Loved One?

ORDER FORM

YES, I want to invest $9.95 in my future and have a personal copy of this book. Send ____ copies of *Marketing Your Books: A Collection of Profit-Making Ideas for Authors and Publishers.*

____ I know it's important to promote my book but I'm too busy. I'd like to learn more about the Rosses' consulting service, About Books, Inc.

Please **add $2 per book for postage and handling.** Colorado residents include 7% state sales tax. (Canadian orders must be accompanied by a postal money order in U.S. funds.) Allow 30 days for delivery. Send check payable to: Communication Creativity, Box 909, Buena Vista, CO 81211. Credit card orders may be called to (719) 395-8659

Name _____ Phone (___)_____

Address _____

City _____ State ____ Zip _____

Here's my check/money order for $ _____

Bill my __ VISA __ MasterCard Expires _____

Acct. #_____ Signature _____

QUANTITY ORDERS INVITED
For bulk discount prices please call (719) 395-8659

Turn Page for More Valuable Marketing & Publishing Tools!

More Valuable Time Saving, Money Making Vehicles

_____ I want John Kremer's remarkable new book-selling tool, *1001 Ways to Market Your Books*. $19.95

_____ Send me the Ross's newly revised and expanded paperback edition of *The Complete Guide to Self-Publishing: Everything You Need to Know to Write, Publish, Promote, and Sell Your Own Book* for $16.95.

_____ I want to showcase my ideas in newspapers. Send me the one-of-a-kind directory, *National Survey of Newspaper "Op-Ed" Pages*. $14.95

_____ I'm interested in doing a book about my area. Mail me a copy of *How to Make Big Profits Publishing City and Regional Books*. $14.95

_____ I'm really serious about selling my books. Send me information about Marilyn and Tom's highly recommended 6-hour cassette tape program, *Book Promotion and Marketing: Success Strategies to Increase Your Sales*. $69.95

_____ I want information on more books on publishing and marketing. Here is a SASE with 45 cents postage. Send the Maverick Mail Order Bookstore catalog.

Communication Creativity

425 Cedar Street • P.O. Box 909
Buena Vista, CO 81211